Daoism in China

Written by Wang Yi'e
Translated by Zeng Chuanhui
Edited by Adam Chanzit

CHINA INTERCONTINENTAL PRESS

TABLE OF CONTENTS

PREFACE

Daoism is considered by many scholars to be the least understood of the world's major religions. Many people think the term "Daoism" only signifies the philosophical school of Laozi and Zhuangzi. In fact, Daoism is an intellectual, spiritual, and folk tradition that in different times and regions has taken on very different meanings.

Not only has Daoism taken on many different forms over its long history, it also has received the influence of early Chinese spirituality and Confucianism, as well as Buddhism and other religions originally foreign to China, making it difficult to precisely define Daoism as any kind of unified philosophy, religon, or set of folk customs. Understanding general trends of Daoism is no easy task for a Chinese person; it is even more difficult for a non-Chinese person, because the development of Daoism is inseparable from that of Chinese culture. It seems a non-Chinese person must first broaden his or her conceptions of "philosophy" and "religion" in order to grasp the essentials of Daoism.

This book was translated through the cooperation of a Chinese and an American scholar. We are fortunate to have had the opportunity to work together, drawing on each other's knowledge and understanding of our own cultures. A Chinese specialist's knowledge is crucial to understanding the complexities of the classical Chinese of the ancient Daoists, while an English speaker more familiar with an average English reader's knowledge and mindset, can help elucidate these often complex concepts to a non-Chinese audience.

Translating between Chinese (especially classical Chinese) and English is a difficult task and requires much choice on the part of a translator. One choice we were often faced with, for example, concerns translating names of Daoist sects, mountains, temples, and deities. We opted to translate some names directly into English if we thought they might be of interest to a reader; or helpful to his or her understanding; however, sometimes there is no good translation of a mountain or deity, and simply using pinyin at least avoids misleading the reader. For certain critical concepts without a translation we considered satisfactory, we use the pinyin and add an explanation. On a deeper level, it is important to note that in classical Chinese, one Chinese character often has multiple meanings, allowing for ambiguity crucial to Daoist rhetoric; often when translating these texts into English, the meaning becomes too specific, too narrow. The translator then must find a way to best express the original meaning (or meanings), but when it comes to translating from classical Chinese into English, much is inevitably "lost in translation." Some translation inevitably comes down to choice and taste and we hope the reader will benefit from our good choices and forgive our weaker ones.

It is also important to note that this book was originally written for a Chinese audience, and in the original edition many sections assume cultural and historical knowledge that an average, educated non-Chinese person would not have. Therefore we often added material (and a few times omitted material) in order to clarify points and make the book more readeable for a non-Chinese person.

The first three chapters help situate Daoism within the

context of Chinese history and trace its development. This is probably the most crucial section of the text for someone seeking a brief answer to the question: "What is Daoism?" The contents of the fourth chapter regarding Daoist deities cannot be fully retained with one read; hopefully interested readers, however, will develop a sense of the vast Daoist pantheon. The fifth and sixth chapters contain detailed information concerning sacred temples and mountains. While the information may be in too much detail for some readers, it could be of interest to those wishing to travel in China. Visitors to Daoist temples or sacred Daoist mountains might find it a handy guide.

The final three chapters convey a sense of the state of Daoism today. It is important to realize that much of the Daoist intellectual tradition as well as its cultivation techniques are transmitted from master to disciple, while its more popular movements flourish outside of large cities. Therefore knowledge of organizations and their activities does not equate to a complete understanding of the scope of contemporary Daoism. Readers may particularly enjoy the section in the final chapter concerning the influence of Daoism on traditional Chinese festivals.

We hope this book will pique readers' continued interest in Daoism, whether through further reading, climbing the five sacred mountains, or even personal cultivation. As the modern literary giant, Lu Xun, once remarked, "Daoism is the root of Chinese culture. Using the perspective of Daoism, many difficult enigmas can be unravelled in an instant." The study of Daoism is an excellent way to penetrate the depths of Chinese culture, and can broaden our perceptions and aid us in our daily lives.

Zeng Chuanhui and Adam Chanzit

August 3, 2004

World Religions Institute,

Chinese Academy of Social Sciences, Beijing, China.

INTRODUCTION

When writing an introduction to Chinese religion, one must first discuss Daoism, because it is the only religion to have adopted the spiritual traditions of early China. China is a multiethnic nation with many religions. Among the five major religions existing in modern times, Daoism, Buddhism, Catholicism, Protestantism, and Islam, only Daoism is indigenous to China. The cosmology of Daoism is consistent with that of ancient Chinese philosophy; its principles, including worship of nature, pursuit of inner purity, and reduction of personal desire, have been important goals for Chinese people for tens of centuries. Daoist images, from paintings to literature of the sublime realms and the immortals inhabiting them, have spread throughout China and have been passed on from generation to generation. The tradition has become so widespread that much of the content of Daoist belief has evolved into common practice and is seen as folk custom. Foreign religions which have come to China, have thus inevitably been influenced by Daoism, even as they penetrate Chinese culture.

Religious Daoism was officially born in the second century CE. It originally took shape as a revolt by the oppressed peasantry, who longed for an ideal, just society. However, it was later molded by religious reformists such as Gehong, Lu Xiujing and Wang Chongyang, and had its most prosperous period from the 7th to the 14th centuries CE becoming, along with Confucianism and Buddhism, one of the three ideological pillars of China. After the 15th century, the mutual influence between the three ideologies increased, blurring distinctions between them. Many people believe in both Buddhism and Daoism, and there are also many common practices that incorporate values from both traditions, as well as Confucianism. Temples and worshippers that are purely Daoist have decreased in modern times, yet the influence of Daoism on Chinese culture remains profound. To this day, there are tens of thousands of Daoist monks, clerics and nuns, and around 4500 Daoist temples. Many Daoist temples are not only sacred places of worship, but also tourist attractions with great historical and cultural value, representing essential traits of Chinese civilization.

This concise introduction to Daoism, authored by Professor Wang Yi'e and published by China Intercontinental Press, offers an overall introduction to the origin, formation, and evolution of Daoism, including information about its doctrines and systems, the compilation of its classics and scriptures, as well as its influence throughout the world. The work not only provides the reader with a basic introduction to Daoism, but also will be helpful in better understanding China and its people.

May many readers enjoy this book!

Zhao Kuangwei

August, 11, 2003

Center for Religious Research, China

CHAPTER 1
SPIRITUALITY IN EARLY CHINA

Among the existing five major religions in China, Buddhism, Daoism, Islam, Catholicism and Protestantism, only Daoism is indigenous to China. Although of these five religions Daoism currently has the least number of temples, its influence on the development of Chinese culture and the daily habits of Chinese people is immense, precisely because it inherited and carried on the earliest spiritual traditions in China. Anywhere in the world where there are Chinese people, one can easily see the influence of Daoism. It is no exaggeration to say that Chinese culture cannot be understood without a proper understanding of Daoism.

The religious Daoist order was formed in the second century during the Late Han Dynasty. However, its doctrines and patterns of thought can be traced back tens of centuries before the Christian era. It is commonly regarded that religious Daoism has three major origins: 1) Ancestor and nature worship originating in primitive society; 2) The doctrines of immortals, the ancient mystics (fangshi) and their occult techniques (fangshu) emerging in the Spring and Autumn and Warring States Periods (roughly the 8th to 3rd centuries BCE) 3) The Huang-Lao School, which flourished in the Han Dynasties from 202 BCE to 220 CE. Huang signifies Huangdi, the Yellow Emperor, the legendary founder of China, while Lao signifies Laozi, the author of the well-known *Daode Jing* and one of the philosophers later termed "Daoist".

1. Ancestor and Nature Worship in Primitive Society

Daoism is a polytheistic religion, many of whose traditions and doctrines were inherited from the people who lived on the land now called "China". Ancestor and nature worship is the belief in spirits of nature and the souls of deceased tribal ancestors. According to archaeological data, the earliest religious consciousness appeared in the late Paleolithic age between one hundred to fifty thousand years ago. In 1933 when archaeologists found Upper Cave Man bones at Mount Dragon Bone (the place where "The Peking Man" was originally discovered), they were astonished to notice that all the skulls were placed in the same direction, and that stone spinning wheels and arrowheads were buried with the skeletons. Some red iron ores, which could only be available several kilometers away, were scattered around the tomb. Yet no such funerary objects were found in fossil sites from earlier periods. This indicates that the Upper Cave Man were the first to have concepts of a world beyond death.

Many archaeological excavations and historical records have

◎ Yuan Dynasty Daoist reliefs (Daochuan County, Shaanxi Province).

demonstrated that the origin of nature worship was directly related to the initiation of agricultural activities. In early times when agricultural technology was still basic, harvests heavily depended on fluctuations of the natural environment. People ascribed every kind of natural phenomenon to various controlling deities, linking all natural changes to the spiritual. If an abundant harvest came, it was a reward from the deities of the natural world; if there was a poor harvest, it was punishment from the spiritual world. Since weather had such a powerful influence on the product of farmers, the sky or "Heavenly" realms were seen as unfathomable and omnipotent. The sun was also commonly worshipped, because it gives light and heat, symbolizes the shift between day and night, and is also related to the four seasons. Due to their vital influence on agricultural activity, other natural elements were also worshipped, such as the moon, stars, wind, thunder, rivers, lakes, seas, plants, and animals. The totem symbols of celestial bodies have been found on sites of excavated relics from the Neolithic age, such as Dawenkou Cultural Site, Tai'an, Shandong Province; Hemudu Cultural Site, Yuyao County, Zhejiang Province; and Majiayao Cultural Site, Lintao County, Gansu Province.

Ancestral worship was predominant in Chinese tradition, probably because in ancient times people had no way to prevent droughts and floods, necessitating the unification of all tribes under the leadership of powerful heroes. These ancient people had such heroes from their own past and worshipped them. Since these heroes were also considered ancestors, this laid the foundation for the Chinese tradition of ancestral worship. The legendary hero-ancestor, Fuxi, and the heroine-ancestor, Nuwa, along with the Three August Ones, and the Five August Emperors, are the earliest figures of this sort. Hero-ancestor worship later extended to all extraordinarily talented and virtuous figures found in history, such as emperors, ministers, generals, scientists, doctors or benefactors. This tradition has also resulted in special emphasis on the virtue of filial piety and burial of the dead, including burying precious belongings with the dead as offerings. As it turns out, this custom helped create rich archaeological resources.

In the Shang Dynasty (roughly 2000 BCE to 1000 BCE), primitive totem and nature worship were replaced by the worship of Heaven (Shangdi) and sacrifice to ancestors. The deities who were believed to represent the will of Heaven were called "shen" or gods, the spirits of the dead ancestors of families and clans were called "gui" or ghosts, and the people who played the role of bridge between deities and people were called "wu" (male witch) or 'xi' (female witch). The great number of excavated oracles from this period proves that divination was performed using bones and tortoise shells. Divination was usually practiced in anticipation of important events, such as wars, sacrifices, hunts, or farming decisions. Oracles were used to foretell the nature of harvests, offspring, wealth, weather and stockbreeding.

The Zhou Dynasty (11th century BCE-1st BCE), which replaced the Shang, inherited its spiritual elements. In the Zhou Dynasty, the celestial and royal powers were even more closely linked; not only did the emperors' orders come from Heaven, but they were even believed to be "Sons of Heaven". They were thought to rule the mundane world on behalf of a "Heavenly Mandate". A strict ritual system stipulated that only Sons of Heaven had the right to sacrifice to all deities. Dukes, on the other hand, might sacrifice to heaven and earth, the sun, moon and constellations, and the mountains in their own dukedoms, while the common people were only allowed to sacrifice to their own ancestors. Historical records of the sacrificial systems, as well as punishment via disease and disaster due to violations are easy to find in such classics as *The Book of History, The Book of Ritual, and The Rites of the Zhou Dynasty*.

Additionally, in the process of founding its religious order, Daoism synthesized many nature and ancestral deities, along with their sacrificial ceremonies, from many minority groups of southwest China.

According to *A Handbook of Daoism* (Zhongzhou Ancient Works Publishing House, Henan, China, 1993), Daoist deities may be classified into eight groups based on their origins: 1) those who evolved from the totem and nature worship of various clans in ancient China; 2) those who evolved from ancestor, hero and sage worship; 3) those of the five sacred mountains (Mount Tai in Shandong, Mount Heng in Hunan,

Mount Hua in Shaanxi, Mount Heng in Shanxi, and Mount Song in Henan) and the four sacred rivers (Yangtze River, Yellow River, Huai River and Jishui River) who came into being during the early stages of the unification of Chinese society from the 3rd century to the 1st century BCE; 4)those of heaven, earth, the four directions, and towns and villages, who emerged from roughly the fifth century to the ninth century CE.; 5) The Three Pure Ones, the supreme Daoist deities, and the Four Imperials, three emperors and one queen who rule the heavenly domain; 6) Deities taken over from Buddhism; 7) Local, folk, and trade deities taken from various areas and nationalities; 8) Sect founders, great masters, immortals who gained eternal life and godlike powers through cultivation, and many famous hermits accumulated over the course of Daoist history.

Thus it can be seen that the pantheon of Daoist deities contains many from the earliest times, as well as those who earned their membership in later chapters of history.

2. Doctrines of Immortals and Occult Masters in the Spring and Autumn and Warring States Periods

The doctrines of immortals also arose from ancient nature and ancestral worship. The doctrines not only propose that there are spirits in our everyday environment as well as ancestral spirits, but also that people can discover medicines to stave off death and can cultivate longevity and gain supernatural powers by consuming elixirs. Once they become immortals, they attain a life free of confinement, discontent, and earthly concern. They can also roam freely between Heaven and Earth.

The immortal doctrines were quite popular in the Warring State Period (475 BCE - 221 BCE). Many descriptions of immortals can be found in books from northern and central China from that time. For example, Zhuangzi calls immortals "shenren" (godlike person), "zhiren" (supreme person), and "zhenren" (perfected person). In the first chapter, "Free and Easy Wandering", he writes: "There is a godlike person living on faraway Guye Mountain, with skin like ice and snow, gentle and shy like a young girl. He doesn't eat the five grains, but inhales the wind, drinks the dew, soars on the clouds and mist, rides a flying dragon, and wanders beyond the four seas."

The famous ancient book *The Classic of the Mountains and Seas* says there is a sacred mountain named Kunlun somewhere in northwest China. It contains splendid palaces, beautiful gardens, various precious flowers, fantastic trees, rare birds and bizarre beasts. The water flowing from the sacred spring could make people live forever. The original ancestors of the Chinese, including the Yellow Emperor and Empress Lei, along with Great King Yu (a hero-ancestor) and the Queen Mother of the West (the head of all goddesses), reside there.

◎ Ming Dynasty glaze ornament, Queen Earth Temple (Jiexiu County, Shanxi Province).

The *Liezi*, also an ancient classic, says there are five sacred mountains in a place named Guixu (returning base) beyond the East China Sea. Their names are: Daiyu (vehicle of Mount Tai), Yuanqiao (round mountain), Fanghu (square kettle), Yingzhou (sea island), and Penglai (peng and lai are names of grass). The height and perimeter of each mountain is 15,000 kilometers, the perimeter of the plains on the peaks is 4,500 kilometers, and the distance across all the islands is 35,000 kilometers. Houses, pavilions, and terraces there are made of gold and jade. The birds and beasts wear silk robes. Pearls, flowers and fruit grow on the trees. Any one who eats of them will never die. Immortals live on the mountains. Their voices echo each other for long distances; they fly up and down to visit each other. The population is countless.

In his great work, *Records of the Historian*, Si-Ma Qian, the foremost historian of the Han Dynasty, gives a more detailed description. He relates the stories of how kings and vassals sent expeditions in search of the three legendary sacred mountains of Penglai, Fangzhang (Fanghu) and Yingzhou. It was told that they were located in the Gulf of Bo Hai, which was not so distant. There one could supposedly find pills of immortality. From a distance, the mountains seemed to be clouds; but when within reach, they were submerged in water. Whenever people were on the verge of accessing the shores, the mountains were blown away or the boats swept back. Hence the mountains were actually unreachable. There are many other classics with similar tales.

Immortals are those with great power, who need not strive or labor, and are free of disease and death. They dance, sing, or drink all day. They dwell in the places where Yin and Yang are perpetually harmonious, the Sun and Moon always shine, seasons are punctual, wind and rain is balanced, boys and girls grow healthy and tall and find a suitable mate, and harvests are abundant.

In most immortal doctrines, the quest for immortality is popular among kings and nobles. A lot of mystics, called "fangshi" ("fang" means outlying area, "shi" means learned person-- "fangshi" arose from outside society), entered society when the times required. They claimed that they had special skills and knowledge of divination, astrology, and medicine, or they knew the road to the sacred mountains. These skills were called "fangshu" ("shu" means technique).

In the beginning, fangshi and fangshu were referred to generally because the distinction between science and magic was not understood. Astronomy and astrology, chemistry and alchemy, medication and exorcism, anything that was out of the ordinary would be ascribed to fangshu. And those who undertook the practices were labeled as fangshi. However, the two terms in historical records refer mostly to the self-claimed masters of immortality. Among them, Changhong, Pengzu, Rongcheng, Xufu, Li Shaojun, and Luanda, were especially famous. In particular, Xufu's story about a journey to the sacred mountains is well-known in China and Japan.

It is said that Xufu was a fangshi in the Qin Dynasty (221 BCE- 206 BCE). After he succeeded in convincing the Emperor of Qin (China's first Emperor), he was sent, along with thousands of virgin boys and girls, to seek immortality pills on the Three Sacred Mountains. But he never returned, leaving an unsolved enigma. Daoism inherited the idea that people could use pills of immortality to become immortals or spirits, and this had great influence over the core beliefs of early Daoists. Over time, Daoism developed and expanded religious customs and doctrines, "outer" and "inner alchemy"[1]playing central roles and becoming important and unique techniques of self-cultivation.

---

[1] "Outer alchemy" refers to two practices: one is the transformation of base metals into precious ones, similar to alchemy in a Western context. The second meaning involves mixing elixirs in order to make pills that stave off death, allowing people to live forever. "Inner alchemy", which developed later, borrowed the terminology and thinking patterns of "outer alchemy". "Inner alchemy" emphasizes cultivation methods in which a practictioner uses his or her basic nature and life force to elevate spirituality and prolong life. The ultimate goal of inner alchemy is to build up a spiritual entity that resembles one's original nature--an entity that can leave the body, transcend the earthly realm, and travel throughout the universe. While to some this may seem somewhat bizarre and abstract, cultivation can be appreciated on many levels; even many basic methods of "inner alchemy" can reward a practitioner with great pleasure, physical benefits, and mental health.

3. Huang-Lao Daoism in the Han Dynasty

The spiritual elements of Daoism were adopted from ancestor and nature worship, and doctrines of the immortals, while its intellectual side came from philosophical Daoism and Huang-Lao Daoism. "Daojia" or "philosophical Daoism" is the title used since the Han Dynasty (206 BCE-220 CE) for the school founded by Laozi and Zhuangzi, great philosophers of the Spring and Autumn and Warring States Periods. According to *Records of the Historian*, Laozi was born around 570 BCE, in Ku County in the state of Chu. Because the characters for Lao and Li were pronounced identically at that time, his surname was mistakenly changed to Li in many historical records. It is said he was the royal historian of the Zhou Dynasty. Having witnessed the disintegration of the dynasty during his old age, he resigned from the court to become a hermit.

Zhuangzi is a major successor to Laozi's doctrine. His lifetime, impossible to verify, is estimated to have taken place around 355 BCE-275 BCE.

Dao is the core concept of Laozi's philosophy. It is the root and essence of all existence in the universe, and is also the origin of the universe. The *Daodejing*, or *Book of Dao and Its Virtue*, says, "Dao emerged before the cosmos. It is solitary, self-grounded, and unchanging, permeating all processes without fail. We can deem it the mother of the world. Look at it and you will not see it, listen to it and you will not hear it. It is shapeless, existing apart from the senses. It is the permanent root from which all things grow."

Zhuangzi developed the philosophy of Laozi, claiming that the Dao is permanent, not something imagined. It permeates everything at every time, although it cannot be directly perceived. It is permanent, infinite and its movement is limitless. The birth, changes and extinction of all things have a temporary nature, yet through their changes they manifest the rules of Dao. He explicates the doctrine that

© Tang Dynasty statue of Laozi.

◎ The Yellow Emperor Inquires of Dao.

The Yellow Emperor is regarded as the founder of Chinese civilization. This picture relates the story of how after uniting the Middle Land of China, and allowing the people to live in peace and prosperity, the Yellow Emperor traveled to Mount Kongdong. On the mountain, he visited Guangchengzi, an early Daoist master, to express his aspiration of availing crops with the vital energy of heaven and earth, and availing the masses through the control of yin and yang.

Dao does all through "wuwei". Wuwei is a crucial concept in Daoist philosophy and religion; it means that one should not impose artificial values when acting, but instead should act in accordance with natural ones, the principles of Dao. Zhuangzi also states that the nature of Dao is supremely good; it produces

everything in natural states, without any idea of owning its deeds, which demonstrates a kind of wuwei. Dao is of the same essence as people, because it is immanent, so the spiritual changes of people express the law of Dao. He concludes that people are of the same essence as everything in the world: "Heaven and earth were born at the same time I was, and the ten thousand things are one with me."

The scholastic fellowship of the Jixia Academy at Linzi, the capital of the state of Qi during the Warring States Period,

◎ Laozi Terrace at Luyi County, Laozi's hometown (Henan Province).

(present day Zibo, Shandong Province) merged Laozi's doctrine with the legendary figure of the Yellow Emperor (Huangdi). The so-called Huang-Lao School is the general name for those who advocated Huang-Lao Daoism. They honored Huangdi and Laozi as the founders of their school, and by linking Laozi with Huangdi, they symbolically elevated the status of their school. They also absorbed some Confucianist, Moist and Legalist thought. Their surviving representative works are *Nine Lords*

(Jiuzhu) now a chapter in *Yiyin* and *The Four Books of Huangdi.*

In the early years of the Western Han Dynasty, the economy of the empire had been damaged severely by long, drawn out wars. In order to redevelop and rehabilitate the people, some politicians such as Zhangliang and Caocan proposed Huang-Lao Daoism as a ruling theory. Lujia, one scholar of that time, used a full chapter to explain wuwei in his book *Xinyu* (new discourses), saying that wuwei is the most distinctive feature of the Dao of Huangdi and Laozi. He concluded, by evaluating historical experience, that the policies of Emperor Yao and Shun in primitive times, and those of the Regent

◎ The Sermon Terrace of Louguantai in Shaanxi, the place where Laozi instructed the *Daode Jing* to Yinxi.

Zhou ostensibly seemed quite passive, but in the end made the whole society prosperous and peaceful. The First Emperor of Qin dominated the country with despotic policies and military force, but his reign quickly crumbled. It is stated in *The Records of the Historian* that when Caocan was the Prime Minister, he respected Gaigong, an expert of Huang-Lao Daoism, as the most honored member of his staff. He managed the country according to Huang-Lao Daoism, produced peace and wealth for the country, and was praised as the "Sage Prime Minister".

In the reigns of Emperor Wen and Jing (179 BCE-141 BCE), productivity developed quickly under the guidance of Huang-Lao Daoism, which promulgated purity and wuwei. Queen Dou, wife of Emperor Wen and mother of Emperor Jing, especially advocated Huang-Lao Daoism. The emperor, prince and other royal relatives often studied the writings of the Huang-Lao School and the philosophy dominated the times.

It was during the time of Emperor Wu, the son of Emperor Jing, that Huang-Lao Daoism became the theoretical foundation for the belief in immortals. Emperor Wu (140 BCE-87 BCE), while upholding Confucianism, was also entranced by the doctrines of immortals. The advocates of these doctrines were eager to establish a theoretical system to campaign against

Confucianism. They naturally looked to Huang-Lao Daoism. On the one hand, Huang-Lao Daoism was quite prevalent at that time; there were some expressions, such as "The Dao of everlasting sight and eternal life", which could be adapted to use. On the other hand, it was only Huangdi and Laozi whose status could

◎ *The Six Gods of the Southern Constellation*, a Ming Dynasty fresco (Jia County, Shaanxi Province).

match those of Yao-Shun and Confucius. Hence Huang-Lao Daoism was gradually applied to the doctrines of immortals, and the two systems eventually merged into one. This system of thought ended up as the foundation of a religion independent of philosophical Daoism, the founder of which, Laozi, was promoted to the Heavens and crowned as an immortal, a deity.

During the Eastern Han Dynasty (25-220 CE), Laozi was

worshipped along with the newly introduced Sakyamuni, from India. According to *The Book of the Late Han Dynasty*, Emperor Huan (132-167 CE) believed in immortals. In 165, delegates were sent to Ku County in Henan Province, the hometown of Laozi, to perform sacrificial rites in memory of Laozi. The next year, the emperor himself offered sacrifice to Laozi in Zhuolong Palace. Laozi was depicted as the manifestation of Dao, a supreme god who created and coexists with the universe.

However, the belief in immortals only existed in the form of personal thought; congregations had not yet been organized. Though they had been theoretically systemized, these doctrines were only popular belief, mixed with other ancient cultural components without obvious delineation. Therefore it had yet to become a fully formed religion.

CHAPTER 2
THE ESTABLISHMENT OF DAOIST ORGANIZATIONS AND THE LINEAGE OF THE CELESTIAL MASTERS

1. The Rise of Early Daoist Organizations

Religious Daoism was officially formed in the 2nd century CE near the end of the Late Han Dynasty. Historians mark the founding of religious Daoism with the creation of the Five Bushels Sect (Wudoumi Dao) by Zhang Daoling (anyone who would join the sect had to agree to pay a tithe of five bushels of rice) and the Supreme Peace Sect (Taiping Dao) by the three brothers Zhangjiao, Zhangbao and Zhangliang. At its height, the Han Dynasty government held great power, but by the second

century it was faltering,
approaching its fall. Ministers
and royal relatives manipulated
the power of the central
government; local garrisons
raised war against each other;
floods and droughts were
ceaseless, farmlands deserted,
and famines omnipresent; chaos
spread throughout the land.
According to the historical
records, in 153 CE, about one
third of the counties were

© Statue of the first Celestial Master.

stricken by floods or locust plagues. Tens of thousands of peasant
families fell into bankruptcy, becoming destitute and homeless.
Much of the society was driven into drastic circumstances, and
peasant rebellions was common. There were more than one
hundred uprisings reported in historical records during the reigns
of Emperor An and Emperor Ling (107-188 CE.)

In such years of upheaval, people yearned for Laozi's ideal
of "order through non-action" to once again become a reality.
They also dreamed they could escape from their plights and have

the life of immortals; some people even wished they could become immortals themselves. So the already prevailing Immortal Doctrines and Huang-Lao Daoism were even more welcomed in this period. Meanwhile, more and more occult practitioners (fangshi) arose: they claimed to have the ability to foretell a person's birth and death, to command ghosts and deities, and discuss social change through astrology. Also during this time, various versions of *The Book of Supreme Peace* (*Taiping Jing*) circulated among the masses: it promised the forthcoming of a new era of supreme peace and prosperity.

According to *The Book of the Han Dynasty*, the earliest version of *The Book of Supreme Peace* was actually two related works, entitled *The Celestial Calendar* and *The Book of the Initiation of the Era of Supreme Peace*, and was compiled by Gan Zhongke from the state of Qi during Emperor Cheng's reign (32-7 BCE) until the end of the Early Han Dynasty. It predicted the collapse of the Han Dynasty, and reported that the Supreme God had already sent an immortal named Chijingzi (Pure Energy Master) to teach the people how to establish a society of great peace to replace the dying Han Dynasty. Subsequently, the local government imprisoned Gan for "obscuring the Emperor and confusing the masses". During the reign of Emperor Ai (7-1 BCE), the last emperor of the Early Han Dynasty, a disciple of Gan, named Xia Huoliang, was sentenced to death by the government because he had inherited and spread *The Book of Supreme Peace*. During the reign of Emperor Shun (125-144 CE), the last years of the Late Han Dynasty, another version of *The Book of Supreme Peace* named *Taiping Qingling Shu*, which means *The Book of Pure Commands of the Supreme Peace* emerged once again among the masses. It is recorded in *The Book of Late Han* that this work was a sacred scripture conferred to Yuji by Quyang Quan. Modern scholars speculate that *The Book of Pure Commands of the Supreme Peace* was the same book as *The Celestial Calendar* and *The Book of Initiation of the Era of Supreme Peace*; the differences, mostly of supplement, came from clandestine transcriptions among folk society for tens of years. These two books, the full texts of which are unfortunately lost, appear only as an abstract in the Daoist Canon compiled during the Ming Dynasty. The abstract of the *The Book of Supreme Peace* was edited by Lu-qiu Fangyuan (? -902) from Suzhou (Jiangsu Province) at the end of the Tang Dynasty. He thought the *Taiping Qingling Shu* was verbose, and inconvenient for readers. He abridged the original seventeen scrolls in each section into one scroll, reducing the original one hundred and seventy scrolls to ten. Fortunately, he gives us a glimpse into the nature of the original; otherwise, we would know next to nothing of the work.

From this abstract, we can see the following points:

First, the *Taiping Qingling Shu* adopted the cosmology of the *Daode Jing*: "Dao generates one. One generates two. Two generates three. Three generates the ten-thousand natural kinds." Dao is the origin of the universe as well as its controller, its driving force, and its end.

Second, it preached the Unification of Heaven and Man, as well as correspondence between Man and Heaven. It also said that anything in the social world, including birth, aging, illness and death, prosperity and adversity, blessing and curses, were correlated with or determined by changes of the celestial bodies.

Third, it preached that people could live forever without death; they could become immortals by cultivating Dao. It offered a set of cultivation methods which are the lengthiest and most detailed contents of *The Book of Supreme Peace*. People are divided into seven groups in this book: godlike people, true people, immortal people, people of Dao, sagely people, virtuous people, common people and slave people. The first three groups can live forever without death. People may elevate themselves to higher levels as long as they continue cultivating Dao. Concerning the cultivation methods, the book suggests that the life of human beings comes from the harmonious co-existence of shen (spirit) and qi (energy). The way to live long is to "store qi" and "unite shen"; one uses shen to accumulate qi, and then lets jing (essence), qi and shen merge into one. The name of this method is "concentration on one".

Finally, it claims to realize the political equality among all persons. It elaborately criticizes the social and economic injustice of the times. It compares the "rich-but-cruel" to rats in granaries, accusing them of monopolizing the granaries and disregarding the life of others. This situation was caused, it claims, by the loss of Dao. It proposed that the rule of Dao would take the people as the foundation; the emperor and ministers could not keep the country in order without the support of common people; the emperor and ministers should work hard day after night, and concern themselves with people's sufferings. In a claimed dialogue between god and the author, it was planned to establish a millennium of "Three Qi Harmony", meaning harmony among Heaven, earth and humanity, harmony among emperor, minister and people, as well as harmony among father, mother, and son.

◎ Two parts of an alchemical diagram, which was painted by a Daoist monk during the Song Dynasty (prior to the 12th century) to illustrate the process of making elixirs.

This kind of ideology would lead to bloody insurrections among farmers a few decades later, during which the earliest Daoist orders were organized. The most formidable rebellions were those of the Five Bushels Sect founded by Zhang Daoling and the Suprme Peace Sect created by the three Zhangs. The central text of these early Daoist orders, along with the *Daode Jing*, was the *Taiping Jing*. Zhang Daoling, otherwise known as Zhangling, was born in the state of Pei (now part of Jiangsu Province) around 34 CE. He once was a local official in Jiangzhou County, Baling Prefecture (now in Chongqing Municipality).

However, he soon resigned to cultivate the art of immortality. Historical records show that he believed in Huang-Lao Daoism; he retreated to Mount Heming to cultivate these beliefs. He claimed he had composed a book of twenty-four chapters under dictation from "the Supreme Master Lao" (Laozi) and began his missionary work in 141 CE. He canonized the *Daode Jing*, deified Laozi as "Lord of Daoism", labeled his followers as "spiritual soldiers", ordained himself as leader, established the twenty-four districts of his followers, and sent sacrificial masters to organize them.

Zhang's major activity was the magic treatment of patients with charmed water (fushui, "fu" means charmed paper, "shui" is water) and penance rituals (huiguo). Fushui was a technique by which the practitioner empowered a piece of paper by using charmed stamps, or a bowl of water by chanting spells. After burning the charmed paper in a bowl and mixing the ashes with water, the patient would drink the solution. The process of Huiguo involved a patient seeking healing, writing out all his or her sins and failures, after which the writing was burned. Sometimes the patient would confess silently in meditation before the gods. Zhang instituted a standard tithe of five bushels of rice for these treatments. In large part due to this system, the Five Bushels

Sect spread rapidly in Sichuan and southern Shaanxi.

Zhang Daoling adapted the early explanation of the *Daode Jing* in *Xiang'er's Commentary on Laozi* to serve his religious goals. It is speculated that Xiang'er is the honorific of Zhang Daoling or his grandson Zhanglu. From the remnant scrolls of this commentary from Mogao Cave in Dunhuang, we can see that it often quoted from *The Book of Supreme Peace*, and has a close relationship to the work in general. Zhang Daoling said in this book that "the One" disperses to become "Qi", while "Qi" coalesces to become the Supreme Master Lao. "The One" is Dao. He personified the philosophical Dao as celestial god Supreme Master Lao. Furthermore, he advised people to perform more benefactions; longevity is the reward for virtues, death is the punishment for crimes; people can live forever if they abide by the commandments and perform good deeds.

When Zhang Daoling died in 156 CE, one of his sons, Zhangheng, succeeded his position. When Zhangheng passed away in 179 CE, Zhanglu, his son, took the post. According to historical records, the Five Bushels Sect further expanded under Zhanglu's rule. He defeated several local powers in southern Shaanxi, gaining control of those regions along with Sichuan. In these regions, he established a theocracy of the Five Bushels

Sect, and titled himself as "Teacher Ruler." His government offered free room along with grains and meat to poor passengers, forbade the slaughter of animals during the first half of the year (because this was considered the period of gestation and child rearing), restricted the production of alcohol, and established a lenient system of justice. According to these laws the punishment for violations of the sectarian prescripts was to build roads as compensation; convictions were made only for people who had offended three times or more. This governance lasted over thirty years, and was heartily welcomed by the people, who lived and labored in peace and contentment.

When Caocao (a Prime Minister, who during the collapse of the Han, actually had more power than the Emperor) raised troops against his mini-state in 215 CE, Zhanglu surrendered, was given the title "Duke Langzhong", and was annointed "General Zhennan" (zhennan means "Guard the South"). Therefore the Five Bushels Sect was able to survive. Zhang Daoling was later honored as "Celestial Master", and Zhanglu as "Heir Master".

The three brothers Zhangjiao, Zhangbao, and Zhangliang were born in Julu, Hebei. They believed in Huang-Lao Daoism. They preached the *Dao Dejing* among the masses, and also secretly spread the Supreme Peace sect. Their methods were similar to those of the Five Bushels Sect, also using "charmed water" techniques. After more than ten years, they had hundreds of thousands of followers scattered throughout the eight eastern prefectures of You, Ji, Qing, Xu, Yang and Yu. These masses erupted in a great rebellion in 184 CE; due to the fact that the followers wrapped yellow cloth around their head, this rebellion has come to be known as the Yellow Turban Rebellion. It was the greatest uprising since the rebellion of Chensheng and Wuguang at the end of the Qin Dynasty. Regional warlords across the country banded together and eventually crushed the uprising. The three Zhang brothers were killed. The Supreme Peace Sect was forbidden to spread; in fact many of its followers converted to the Five Bushels Sect.

Besides the three generations of Zhang Daoling and the three Zhang brothers, there was another founder of a Daoist organization. This was the remarkable Zhangxiu. He originally followed Zhang Daoling, then later established his own religious sect in southern Shaanxi, the rituals of which were quite similar those of the Five Bushels Sect. His group rose up to echo the revolt of the Supreme Peace Sect. Eventually his sect merged with that of Zhanglu.

The formation processes of the Five Bushels Sect and the Supreme Peace Sect prove that the earliest founders were originally disciples of Huang-Lao Daoism. The *Taiping Jing* was their common text. They preached Huang-Lao Daoism to the masses in a turbulent era. They helped poor farmers with healing charms and by curing illnesses. Having gained the heart of a large number of farmers, they organized these followers into Daoist groups. Thus in the earliest Daoist organizations, poor farmers composed the main membership, and their ideology advocated resistance to the cruelty imposed by the ruling class. These smaller groups soon merged into the Five Bushels Sect.

2. The Lineage of the Celestial Masters

Because Zhang Daoling was honored as "Celestial Master" after the Jin Dynasty (third century CE), the Five Bushels Sect eventually became known as the Celestial Master Sect. "Celestial Master" also became the hereditary title for Zhang's successors. From the Tang Dynasty (since the 7th century CE) to modern times, this title has been the symbol of the highest authority in the Zhengyi Sect (further explained in Chapter 3), and throughout history has been recognized by Emperors as well. In the history of feudal China, only two family lines have been so honored unanimously from dynasty to dynasty, no matter the chaos of war or changes of regime. One is that of the Confucian Sages in Qufu, Shandong,Province, and the other is that of the Celestial Masters in Mount Dragon and Tiger, Jiangxi Province.

According to the Annals of Mount Dragon and Tiger, the succession of the Celestial Masters was strictly stipulated: the Celestial Mastership "may not be transferred to a brother if any son exists; may not be transferred to a grandson if any brother exists; may not be transferred to a brother-in-law if any grandson exists; may not be transferred to a nephew if any brother-in-law exists; may not be transferred to an uncle if any nephew exists; may not be transferred to any other family member if any uncle exists; may not be transferred to a non-family member if any family member exists". There are three testimonial objects: the book of twenty-four scrolls given by Laozi, the charm seal of Governor Yangping and the sword for slaying demons also given by Supreme Master Lao. There had been sixty-three generations in this lineage before 1949, called "The Lineage of the Celestial Master of the Han Dynasty." This lineage ended in 1969 when the last heir passed away in Taipei, leaving no offspring.

It is interesting to note that while Zhang Daoling's hometown is not Guixi (in Jiangxi), Confucius' hometown is Qufu (Shandong Province), where the lineage of Confucian Sages has always been located. According to the Daoist scripture, *The Lineage of Celestial Masters of the Han Dynasty*, in the years during Emperor He's reign (88-105 CE), Zhang visited all of the famous sacred places for cultivation, until finally he and his disciple, Zhaochang, came to Mount Yunjin (Brocade Cloud Mountain) in Guixi County under the guidance of two fairy cranes. Attracted by its elegant scenery and its wise and powerful residents, he

◎ The Celestial Master Mansion, the founder temple of the Zhengyi Denomination (Mount Dragon and Tiger, Jiangxi Province).

stopped to make elixirs. After three difficult years, he was rewarded with elixirs, and a dragon and a tiger appeared before him. From then on, this mountain was called Mount Dragon and Tiger. It is from this mountain that Zhang Daoling began his missionary journey, which eventually lead to the founding of religious Daoism. After surrendering to Caocao, Zhanglu and some of his followers were transferred to the areas around Luoyang and Yecheng in Henan. When Zhangsheng, son of Zhanglu, took over the sect, Caocao offered him grains (a kind of currency at that time) and protection, but Zhangsheng declined the offer, and returned with the sword and seal passed down from Zhang Daoling to Guixi (present day Jiangxi Province), where the Lineage of the Celestial Masters has settled ever since.

Since Guixi in Jiangxi was the birthplace of Daoism, many Daoist relics have been preserved there. Among them, the most important attractions are True Unity Temple and Supreme Pure Temple on Mount Dragon and Tiger, as well as the Celestial Master Mansion at the foot of the mountain. Zhengyi Temple was built at the place where Zhang Daoling made elixirs, but the earliest date of its construction remains unknown. Throughout history it has been a place for disciples to offer sacrifice to Zhang Daoling. Daoist priests come to worship him, leaving many hymns dedicated to their spiritual leader. The formal monastic buildings were built around the tenth century CE. According to the existing stele in front of Celestial Master Temple on Mount Dragon and Tiger, construction on the temple took place in the Baoda Era (742-755 CE) of the Southern Tang Dynasty in the Five Dynasties and Ten States Period; during the Song Dynasty it underwent several expansions and repairs. Having been further enlarged during the Ming Dynasty, it received its present name, "True Unity Temple". During the Qing Dynasty, this temple was a compound with three buildings, occupying 20 hectares. The offspring of Celestial Master Zhang were supposed to live here to burn incense and worship. Unfortunately, it was destroyed by a fire in the 1940s, leaving only the foundation.

Supreme Pure Temple, about eight kilometers from Supreme Pure Village, is the place where past generations of Celestial Masters held ceremonies. It is said that there once was a thatched cottage wherein Zhang Daoling performed exorcisms, therefore according to Daoist teachings, it is also the place where deities and ghosts accepted the appointments of new Celestial Masters. Zhangsheng originally set up an altar in this temple for conferring his charms and ordaining his disciples. Since then there have been annual assemblies for "Charm-Delivery" and "Priesthood-Ordination" on specified days. Fires and floods damaged these buildings, but they were restored and even expanded countless times during the Song, Yuan, Ming and Qing Dynasties. The temple was formally renamed "Supreme True Unity Temple" in 1114 CE in the third year of Emperor Huizong's reign during the Song Dynasty.

Celestial Master Mansion was the living compound of the Celestial Masters from generation to generation. It is in Supreme Pure Village at the foot of Mount Dragon and Tiger. It is one of several existing residence palaces in China, bearing the title of "The First Home in Southern China". It is said that construction began in the twelfth century CE, during the Song Dynasty. Having undergone much reconstruction, the existing buildings, of which major portions remain from the Qing Dynasty, include a gate, central hall, meditation hall, ceremonial hall, library and garden. The buildings take various shapes of storied houses, platforms, large halls and penthouses; the pillars, girders, walls and roofs are decorated with frescos and sculptures; the old, sky-high trees shade the yards like woods; a brook flows alongside the gate, where there is a vertical tablet on which is inscribed the characters: "Mansion of Heirs to the Celestial Master of the Han Dynasty". The central hall is the office of the Celestial Masters; the meditation hall is the living compound of the Celestial Masters' families, with frontal rooms, wing rooms, and corridors; the ceremonial hall is the sacrificial shrine of the Celestial Masters and their families, where the statues of major Daoist deities as well as Zhang Daoling were enshrined. It is said that the sword and seal kept in the Mansion are those passed down from Zhang Daoling.

CHAPTER 3
THE DEVELOPMENT OF DAOISM AND THE FORMATION OF SECTS

1. From the Celestial Masters to Zhengyi Daoism

Over nearly two thousand years of Daoist development, many denominations and sects came into being due to differences in interpretations of teachings, systems of heredity, and methods of organizing and forming institutions. There are eighty-six denominations and sects recorded in documents at White Cloud Temple in Beijing. After the 15th century, more eclectic sects emerged among the people because of Daoist intercourse with Confucianism and Buddhism. Among these numerous sects, some were named after a famous master from history, some after the sect's place of origin, some after a Daoist scripture they followed, and some after a cultivation method. However, throughout history there were only four widely recognized denominations--and these can be categorized into branches: Zhengyi Daoism (Orthodox Unity Daoism) and Quanzhen Daoism (Complete Realization Daoism).

Zhengyi Daoism evolved directly from the Celestial Masters Way. In the middle of the 3rd century CE, central China was

© The Azure Cloud Temple of Mount Tai.

reunited after years of war and chaos. The Celestial Master Way began to develop in two directions: on the one hand, it continued to spread widely among poor farmers, emerging as organizations fighting against the ruling class' oppression. Among the numerous insurrections in the name of Daoism, the one lead by Sun'en and Luxun during the 3rd century was the largest. When these rebellions were thoroughly squashed, Daoism lost much of its original influence over farmers. On the other hand, many nobles began to follow the Celestial Masters Way. The world of immortals proposed by Daoism, rather than notions of an equal society, sparked the interest of many nobles. A lot of intellectuals entered Daoist spheres, carrying with them their personal spiritual pursuits; many wrote new explanations of Daoist tenets in their books, and adjusted many Daoist ceremonies. Thus a period of Daoist reformation took place, with thinkers like Gehong (284-364 CE, Eastern Jin Dynasty), Kou Qianzhi (365-448 CE, Northern Wei Dynasty), Lu Xiujing (406-477 CE, Song Dynasty), and Tao Hongjin (456-536, Liang Dynasty) leading the way.

The inner and outer chapters of *Baopuzi* (*The Master Who Embraces Simplicity*) by Gehong were canonized by later Daoists as major theoretical works. He shifted Daoist ideology from millenarian salvation to personal delivery and immortality. He argued eloquently for the existence of immortals and the possibility of immortality through cultivation, and meticulously itemized various methods of cultivation and alchemy. He also re-annotated Daoist theology according to

Confucian thought, argued Daoist cultivation practice was consistent with Confucian morality, and accepted Confucian norms of righteous words and deeds as being a necessary precondition of cultivation. Thus nobles and intellectuals welcomed his work.

Kou Qianzhi lived in the years during the split between the

◎ The Chanting Ceremony in Laolu Hall (White Cloud Temple, Beijing).

Southern and Northern Dynasties. Under support from imperials and nobles of the Northern Dynasty, he claimed he was visited by Supreme Master Lao, who gave him the title of Celestial Master, along with the *New Musical Liturgy of Commandments from the Clouds* (clouds represent the heavenly realm), a twenty scroll classic. He courageously reformed the teachings of the Celestial Masters Way during the Northern Dynasty, rectified its organizations, instituted liturgical and musical rules, compiled scriptures, and subsequently established the New Celestial Masters Way in the capital city of Pingcheng (now Datong in Shanxi) during the Northern Wei Dynasty. He realized the unification of Daoism with feudal power. His religion was also called the "Northern Celestial Masters Way".

Lu Xiujing lived in Southern China. His major contribution was to inherit and develop Gehong's theories and apply them to the reformation of existent Daoist organizations. He collected large numbers of Daoist scriptures and improved liturgies. His

◎ The Highest Sky Palace (Mount Mao, Jiangsu Province).

reformed Daoism was called the "Southern Celestial Masters Way".

Tao Hongjing also inherited Gehong's theories. He enriched and developed Daoist cosmology on the basis of Laozi and the *Yijing* (*Book of Changes*). He was among the earliest advocates for the unification of Confucianism, Buddhism and Daoism. In his book, *Catalogue of the Daoist Pantheon*, he arranged various Daoist deities into a great hierarchical system for the first time, and promoted the unification and systematization of Daoist theories.

In 364 CE during the Eastern Jin Dynasty, Yangxi, a Daoist priest, claimed that the goddess Madam Wei gave him a 31-scroll scripture called *The True Book of Shangqing* and founded the Shangqing Sect (Shangqing translates as "Supreme Purity"). This sect took *The True Book of Shangqing* as its central text, promoted the Heavenly King of the Origin and Supreme Master Lao as its highest celestial gods, and adopted the "cunxiang" as its chief method of cultivation. By this method, a cultivator can guide celestial gods into his or her body and communicate with the gods of his or her internal organs. These gods report the practitioner's behavior to the celestial gods, who in turn raise or lower the practitioner's status. Followers continue in this way until they are ready to ascend to Heaven as an immortal. This sect spread on Mount Mao in Jiangsu Province.

There are some Daoists who have chosen the Sacred Jewel Scriptures as their central texts. This tradition is the called Lingbao Sect (Lingbao translates roughly as "sacred jewel"). Its main characteristics include declaring universal salvation, paying special attention to liturgies and rituals, and emphasizing moral conversions. Its most sacred mountain is Mount Gezao in Jiangxi Province.

Other Daoist sects, such as the Pure Bright (Jingming) Sect, the Highest Heaven (Shenxiao) Sect, the Dragon Tiger (Longhu) Sect, the Wudang Sect (originated at Mount Wudang), and the Pure Beauty (Qingwei) Sect, continued to emerge throughout the Jin, Tang, and Song Dynasties. They coexisted and studied from each other. This condition changed in 1304, during the Yuan Dynasty when the Emperor granted the honor of "Orthodox Unity Lord" (Zhengyi Lord) to the 38th generation Celestial Master, whose name was Zhang Yucai, and ordered him to command all Daoist sects in China. Since then, Southern and Northern Celestial Master Sects, the Shangqing Sect, and the Lingbao Sect, have been generally called Zhengyi Daoism. Their common characteristics include: they take Zhengyi classics as their central scriptures; they undertake liturgy and exorcist rituals as their major religious services; their clerics are allowed to marry and have children; they are not forced to live in temples and lead a monastic life; and their commandments generally are not particularly strict. Zhengyi Daoism, the general name for all kinds of talismanic sects headed by Mount Dragon and Tiger, formed after Daoism had already entered a relatively mature stage. Among the sects in this denomination, some have preserved their own unique tenets and liturgies, whilst others have conformed to Zhengyi norms.

2. *Quanzhen Daoism*

It used to be claimed that the Quanzhen Denomination of Daoism had a very long history, originating from the celestial god "Royal Lord of the East", and descending from Zhong Lihan and Lu Dongbin (both of whom were ancient Chinese ancestor-heroes). In fact, its origin came significantly later: it was set up by a Daoist named Wang Chongyang around the 12th century CE. Wang Chongyang was born in Xianyang, Shaanxi, in 1113. It was a time of migration and reconfiguration of ethnic populations and cultures in Northern China. The North Song Dynasty was quickly replaced by the Jin Dynasty, established by the Nuzhen minority from North Asia. Daoism, as an ancient aboriginal Chinese culture, was confronted with foreign culture and religious thought; the complicated ethnic and social tensions demanded new doctrines and new canons. Hence arose a new denomination quite different from Zhengyi Daoism.

Wang Chongyang claimed that in 1159 CE at a place called Gahe, he encountered the Immortal Lu Dongbin, who offered

◎ Double Yang Palace (Hu County, Shaanxi Province)

him divine drink, and taught him Daoist truth. Wang immediately left his family for Mount Zhongnan to cultivate Dao. In 1167 CE, he left the mountain, moved eastwards, arrived at the coast in Shandong, and began his missionary work of organizing an order. He recognized his foremost seven disciples, Mayu, Sun Bu'er, Tan Chuduan, Liu Chuxuan, Qiu Chuji, Wang Chuyi and Hao Datong, and established the earliest Quanzhen groups in Wendeng, Ninghai, Fushan, Dengzhou and Laizhou, all in Shandong Province. The names of the five original orders are: Three Religions Seven Jewels Society, Three Religions Golden Lotus Society, Three Religions Three Constellations Society, Three Religions Jade Flower Society, and Three Religions Equal

Society. "Three religions" refers to the ultimate unity of Daoism, Confucianism, and Buddhism. The influence of these societies was great and followers grew quickly in number.

Wang Chongyang adopted songs in sermons to make his ideas more understandable and acceptable among the masses. The collections of his writings and poems compiled by his disciples include the following: *Collection of Chongyang on Perfect Realization* (twelve scrolls), *Collection of Chongyang's Instructions* (three scrolls), *Chongyang's Fifteen Treatises on the Establishment of Daoism*, and *Chongyang's Twenty-Four Oral Teachings for Danyang*. Wang Chongyang also established a set of innovative religious theories and practices by developing the original Daoist doctrines of salvation, contentment in poverty and abstinence. He deemed Daoism to be identical with Buddhism and Confucianism in nature and origin, all of which are true but different in name. He summarized the tenets of his Neo-Daoism as "the unification of the three religions"; he believed that only through such unification can the right path be found. An even more crucial meaning of the term Quanzhen is "du quan qi zhen", which means that a follower should, through detachment from worldly temptations, preserve his or her true nature. Quanzhen is often translated as

"All True", "Complete Truth" or "Complete Realization," but here we will use the original Quanzhen.

First, Wang requested his converts study not only Daoist scriptures such as the *Daode Jing* and *The Book of Pure Silence*, but also the *Heart Sutra* of Buddhism and *The Filial Classic* of Confucianism. He deemed Daoism, Buddhism and Confucianism to be preachers of the same truth, like three branches on one tree.

Second, he combined commandments and teachings of Daoism, Confucianism and Buddhism to establish the fundamental principles of Quanzhen Daoism. In Chongyang's Fifteen Treatises on the Establishment of Daoism, he prescribed the general rules of cultivation and behavioral standards in fifteen categories: 1) Monastic Life, which demands all Quanzhen monks to live collectively in monasteries; 2) Spiritual Wanderings, which demands that Quanzhen Daoists often visit other mountains and temples to pay homage to sacred places and persons, and to learn from other monks; 3) Literary study, which demands that Daoists read classical works, not necessarily in great number, but in great depth; 4) Medicinal study, which demands that Daoists master medicine, otherwise it is impossible to understand the Dao; 5) Shelter of Dao, which requests Daoists live in huts instead of

◎ The Statue of Founder Master Qiu, White Cloud Temple in Beijing. Founder Master Qiu's name is Qiu Chuji, styled "Changchunzi" (Eternal Spring Master), was born in Xixia County, Shandong Province. He followed Master Wang Chongyang in cultivating Dao, and founded the Dragon Gate Sect of Quanzhen Daoism. In his eighties, he traveled to a snowy mountain in central Asia to meet Genghis Khan, and persuaded him to worship Heaven and love people instead of wage war.

large buildings, however this point was forgotten by his disciples soon after his death when the denomination developed well under support from emperors and nobles, allowing many monks to live in palace-like monasteries; 6) Partnership, which demands that Daoists choose virtuous, wise and inspiring partners for cultivation; 7) Meditation, which demands that the mind of a person in meditation be as quiet and stable as Mount Tai, free from any worldly concerns; 8) Mind taming, which demands that those who meditate eliminate distracting ideas; 9) Refining Original Character, which demands Daoists have a gentle temperament; 10) Five-Element Matching, by which the cultivator guides the qi of the five internal organs into harmonious intercourse; 11) Blending of Xing and Ming, the purpose of which is to make xing (original nature) and ming (vital energy) rely on and promote each other; 12) Sacred Way, which guides followers to cultivate in harsh conditions for many years and to accumulate the power to transcend to Heaven; 13) Transcendence from Three Realms, which is to transcend the realms of desire, the material world, and finally, the void; 14) True Body Cultivation, which is the cultivation of the body's original nature; 15) Breaking From the Mundane, which means not to physically leave the mundane world in pursuit of longevity, but to leave it mentally whilst one's body inhabits it.

Third, he synthesized Daoist theories of inner alchemy with Zen Buddhist concepts, denied the importance of theories and words, and concentrated on cultivation practices. He assumed that what is fundamental to cultivating and realizing Dao was a person's unchangeable and genuine nature. He advocated reaching the pure and quiet realm by "understanding one's mind and discovering one's original nature".

Fourth, Wang Chongyang established an overall system of communal religious life in the Quanzhen order, borrowing greatly from Buddhism.

In 1170 CE, Wang Chongyang died in Kaifeng, Henan Province. His Disciples, Mayu and Tan Chuduan took over the management of the Quanzhen Denomination. The seven top disciples founded sects of their own: Mayu, honored as "Danyangzi" (Yang Elixir Master), set up the Immortal Encounter Sect; Tan Chuduan, honored as "Changzhenzi" (Eternal Perfect Master), founded the Southern Emptiness Sect; Hao Datong, honored as "Guangningzi" (Broad Peace Master), founded the Mount Hua Sect; Wang Chuyi, honored as "Yuyangzi" (Yang Jade Master), founded the Mount Yu Sect; Liu Chuxuan, honored as "Changshengzi" (Master of Long Life), established the Mount Sui Sect; Sun Bu'er, wife of Mayu, set up the Pure Silence Sect. As a female disciple, her works which dealt with cultivation methods for women, are the major guides for female cultivators; Qiu Chuji, honored as "Changchunzi" (Eternal Spring Master), established the Dragon Gate Sect. With recognition and support from Genghis Khan, Dragon Gate Sect (Longmen Pai) eventually became the most influential group, to which most Quanzhen temples in Mainland China, Hong Kong, Macao, Taiwan and

Southeast Asia are ascribed. The current headquarters of the China Taoist Association is located in White Cloud Temple in Beijing, which is respected as the founding temple of the Dragon Gate Sect.

While Wang Chongyang was establishing Quanzhen Dao in Northern China, the Southern School of Alchemy, which also claimed to trace its history back to Zhong Liquan and Lu Dongbin, was spreading in southern China under the rule of the Southern Song Dynasty. They made inner elixirs by refining and concentrating essence, energy and spirit through the three processes of physical cultivation, energy cultivation, and spiritual cultivation. Li Daochun, the founder of this group, borrowed from Confucianism and Buddhism and worked them into a Daoist framework. He deemed that the ideals of cultivation in all three ideologies were essentially identical in that they could not exist without "central harmony". Thus he affirmed the inner alchemical method of "central harmony". He integrated some Chan (Zen) theories and methods such as meditation, Gatha [1], and Bang and Bawl [2], and established his own sect. After the collapse of

---

[1] Sanskrit word, meaning writing or chanting poems or songs, used to demonstrate one's level of enlightenment.
[2] A method of passing wisdom: when a seeker of truth asks a question of a Master, the Master beats the student or shouts at the student causing reason to momentarily disappear and ideally resulting in sudden enlightenment.

the Southern Song dynasty in 1279, Quanzhen groups spread into Southern China, and Li Daochun claimed that the Southern School of Alchemy originally belonged to the Quanzhen Denomination. Li Daochun along with the four masters prior to him are honored as the "Five Southern Masters."

In their daily lives, Quanzhen monks wear dark robes, and grow long hair that is kept in a wispy bun, topped with a Daoist cap. Monks and nuns dress in the same style. Daoists have

◎ Daoist ceremonial robe and the Hunyuan hat with a lotus top.

especially prescribed costumes for ceremonies, in which the major players in the rituals have embroidered, colored robes. Zhengyi Daoist priests have similar wear to those of Quanzhen monks in ceremonies and rituals, while their daily dressings are quite plain, bearing little difference from common people. They also do not need to have long hair and can shave. Zhengyi Daoist priests are not forced to keep a vegetarian diet, though they may not eat dog meat or beef, because they believe dogs are a symbol of fidelity and oxen and bulls are a farmer's aids.

There were once other Daoist sects in Chinese history, among which the most famous were Taiyi (Great Unity) Daoism, and Zhenda (True Great) Daoism. However, they died out; only the Zhengyi Dao and Quanzhen Dao Denominations have survived.

CHAPTER 4   DAOIST DEITIES

1. What are Daoist Deities?

Deities, also called immortals, are the basic objects of Daoist faith. They are the personification of Dao, which is the origin and essence of the universe, as well as the ultimate goal pursued by Daoists. According to Daoism, deities are somewhat similar to human beings in appearance, so they are called Sacred Persons, Immortal Persons, Supreme Persons and Perfected Persons, and are like people who have realized truth. However, in many respects they are of course quite different from common people.

First of all, deities have the essence of the origin of the universe or original qi, because they either arose from the origin of the universe and are thus an incarnation of original qi, or they have returned to such a state through cultivation. Second, deities

(immortals) do not die because their lives are identical with Dao. They are the models of Daoists; they also are the model of common people, inspiring them to cultivate in pursuit of reaching the highest realm of "long life without death." Third, deities have powers surpassing common people, such as speeding across the sky, controlling the course of wind and rain, and determining people's blessings and curses. They can dominate everything on earth. People must obey their will or they will incur punishment. Fourth, the celestial world they live in is similar to the mundane world in that it has a strict hierarchical order and management systems. Every deity must maintain his or her duty and obey his or her superior. Fifth, deities have clear division of labor in terms of overseeing the mundane world. They have missions to convert people, give moral instruction using literature, perform

◎ The Pure Jade
Emperor. This is a
ceremonial picture
hung on an altar
during liturgies.

benefactions and exorcisms, etc. Therefore Daoists not only see immortals as ideal role models, but also as protectors of the human race.

Most deities live on heaven, but some inhabit the mundane world. The places dominated by deities are called "Sacred Abodes and Blessed Lands". There are ten Major Sacred Abodes and thirty-six Minor Abodes, where all affairs are managed by immortals sent from Heaven; there are seventy-two Blessed Lands where perfect persons from Heaven, whose celestial ranks are inferior to immortals, manage all other affairs. These places are believed to be perfect places of cultivation, where many famous Daoists dwelt, cultivated Dao, and achieved immortality. There are usually Daoist temples and Daoist relics at these locations. They are the sacred places of Daoism.

Immortal persons and perfect persons are two titles for deities with different ranks. Throughout history, there were various statements concerning the deities' hierarchy. The Supreme Peace Books divided deities into six categories. Gehong's *The Master Who Embraces Simplicity (Baopuzi)* divided them into three categories, and *Supreme Perfect Liturgies* into nine. Here we approximately group them into celestial gods, constellation gods, territorial gods and vagabond gods. There are many deities in Daoism, and for the newcomer to Daoism, becoming clear concerning all the deities and their purposes is overwhelming. Hopefully this chapter will at least give the reader a sense of the scope of Daoist deities and some of their characteristics.

2. Introduction to Daoist Deities

The supreme gods in Daoism are the Three Pure Ones: "The Pure Jade Heavenly Sage of Pre-Existence", "The Heavenly Sage of the Supreme Pure Lingbao (sacred jewel)" and "The Heavenly Sage of Dao and its Virtues in the Shangqing (supreme pure) Realm". In Daoist history it was only after the 9th century that Daoists worshipped the "Three Pure Ones" as the highest celestial gods. In early Daoism, The Sovereign Pure Realm, Supreme Pure Realm and Great Pure Realm were simply the three highest celestial realms ruled by many celestial gods, rather than particular deities. During Tang Emperor Wuzong's reign (841-846), the "Heavenly Sage of the Primordial Origin", "The Great Master of Supreme Dao" and "The Great Master of Supreme Lao" were deified as the highest celestial gods; "The Heavenly Precious Master of the Sovereign Pure Realm", "The Sacred Precious Master of the Supreme Pure Realm" and "The Holy Precious Master of the Great Pure Realm", who are called "The Three Precious Masters", were the second highest celestial gods.

After the 12th century, the highest celestial deities and the "Precious Masters" were gradually incorporated into one set of three deities, while the secondary Three Pure Gods were transformed into the Three Pure Realms where the three highest gods dwell. [①]

The Heavenly Sage of the Origin, also called the Pure Jade Emperor, is the highest of the Three Pure Ones, living in the Sovereign Pure Realm. He is the creator of the universe, and was born before its origin. He is composed of primordial qi, and is eternal and imperishable. He applied Dao when constructing the Universe. He is the symbol of Dao. His statue is usually placed on the middle altar in the Three Pure Ones' Hall of a temple, taking the shape of an old man with a shining circle behind his head and a colorful robe on his body. He either holds a red elixir pill in one hand, or his left hand shows the motion of picking something up (though still empty), while his right hand is also empty. This symbolizes the first stage of Daoist cosmology when it was chaotic, shapeless and void-like. The Winter Solstice is the festival honoring his birth.

The Heavenly Sage of the Lingbao, also called the Supreme

[①] If keeping the rankings and duties of the deities clear seems overwhelming, one should not be overly concerned; a thorough understanding of the seemingly countless deities is not necessary to a basic comprehension of the Daoist religion.

Master of Dao or the Supreme Great Emperor, lives in the Supreme Realm. He is the second ranking of the Three Pure Ones. He was born of congealed vital energy from an auspicious cloud one beautiful morning which impregned his mythical Mother, Madam Hong. He gestated inside her for 3700 years before being born as a human. He is also an embodiment of Dao. His statue is usually placed on the left altar in the Three Pure Ones' Halls, taking the shape of an old man as well. With a Taiji or Ruyi (a S-shape object which is believed to be capable of granting every wish) in hand, his pose symbolizes the second stage of Daoist cosmology when chaos abated to become clear, and yin and yang started to split. It was the state of "One giving birth to two". Daoists honor his birthday on the Summer Solstice.

The Heavenly Sage of Dao and its Virtue, also called Supreme Master Lao, lives in the Supreme Pure Realm. He is believed to be Laozi, founder of the Daoist School during the Spring and Autumn Period. Although originally born before the universe, after his earthly mother swallowed the pure energy of the Sun, she became pregnant with his reincarnated form. He gestated for eighty-one years inside her before being born as a white-haired old man. Thus he was named Laozi, or Old Son. He was given Dao from the first two sages of the Three Pure

Ones, and began to spread Dao among humans. Daoists believe the works of the Three August Ones and the Five Imperial Ones, the founding of religious Daoism by Zhang Daoling, as well as the Daoist reformation by Kou Qianzhi were all conducted under his command. He is commonly recognized as the founder of Daoism. In most iconography, he appears as a white-haired and white-bearded old man, with a Taiji fan or horsetail whisk in his hands. The shrines dedicated to him are called Old Master's Hall or Supreme Pure Hall. If co-worshipped in the Three Pure Ones' Hall, his statue is placed on the right altar.

The Jade Emperor is second only to the Three Pure Ones, and is the general manager of Heaven. He presides over every aspect of the celestial gods. It is believed that he was originally the Celestial God or Supreme God worshipped in early China. Originally, he was a subordinate official of the Heavenly Sage of the Origin, and only attained more importance starting in the Song Dynasty (12th century) when Daoism was becoming more popular and prosperous. In the Ming and Qing Dynasties, he was further elevated to be the sovereign celestial god of folk religion, so there was a saying that "Whilst there is an Emperor on earth, there is a Jade Emperor in Heaven." Daoist scriptures record that there once was a king named King Pure Virtue who

was married to Queen Precious Moon Light. Although they still had no children as they grew old, they continued praying to Heaven. One night, the queen dreamed that the Supreme Master of Dao sent them a golden baby in a carriage. Soon afterwards she became pregnant and gave birth to a son. However when the son matured, he did not succeed

◎ Ming Dynasty wooden statue of the Jade Emperor (White Cloud Temple, Beijing).

to the throne, but instead he retreated to a mountain to cultivate. After innumerable years of cultivation, he finally became the Jade Emperor. The image of the Jade Emperor is similar to that of an emperor of the mundane world. He is black-bearded, appears solemn, and wears a flattop hat with fringes in the front and back. He wears a robe embroidered with a red dragon, and holds a jade tablet.

His wife is the Queen Mother of the West, commonly called Queen Mother. She is believed to be the Essence of the Great

Yin (the Moon). She is in charge of all goddesses in Heaven. Any person who succeeds in realizing Dao and becoming immortal must pay a formal visit to her before the pilgrimage to the Heavenly Sage of Preexistence. She is also the symbol of longevity. The folk tales of Queen Mother's birthday celebration are well known to all Chinese people. In these tales, during the anniversary celebrations in heaven, there is an Immortal-Peach Dinner to entertain guest deities from all directions. Any one who is lucky enough to eat one of the Queen Mother's peaches will live forever. Hence Chinese people often offer peaches as birthday gifts.

The divine rank of the Four Imperial Ones is similar to that of the Jade Emperor. However, since these four deities (three celestial kings and one celestial queen) aid the Jade Emperor, they are also called the Four Auxiliary Ones. They all have separate duties. The first is the Great Emperor of Ziwei Big Dipper. Ziwei, which literally means "Purple Beauty", is the name of the palace he dwells in, but also represents the Big Dipper. It is believed that he is the incarnation of the Heavenly Sage of Preexistence. He only takes orders from the Jade Emperor. His duty is to command all the gods of the constellations and as well as the gods of mountains and rivers, and to control forces of nature such as wind, rain, and thunder. He is also the lord of natural phenomena. During the Song Dynasty, he was so highly esteemed that he was often worshipped together with the Jade Emperor. He also takes the shape of emperors, wearing a flattop hat and dragon robes.

The second of the Four Imperial Ones is the Great Emperor of the Gouchen Constellation. The Gouchen Constellation is the name for the four stars on the left side of the Big Dipper. "Gou" means hook, and describes the shape of the constellation. It is said that the Great Emperor of the Gouchen Constellation inhabits the Gouchen Palace. He presides over all constellations because

◎ Qing Dynasty clay statues of the Four Imperial Ones (White Cloud Temple, Beijing).

of its central location. His image is also that of an emperor.

The third is the Earthly Queen of the Land Gods, abbreviated as Queen Earth. She lives in the Pistil Pearl Palace, and is responsible for the interchange of yin and yang, population growth, and beauty (especially of natural scenery). She is often grouped with the Jade Emperor, and as a pair they are called the "Emperor Heaven and the Queen Earth". The image of Queen Earth is similar to that of ancient Chinese queens. She is affable and elegant, with a phoenix coronet on her head and an embroidered cape draped over her shoulders.

The fourth is the Great Emperor of Longevity of the South Pole. He is also called the Old Immortal of the South Pole or the Constellation of Longevity. His duty is to manage people's life spans. Therefore he is quite loved by people. He has a lumpy forehead, white hair and beard, and generally appears as a gentle and happy old man holding a gnarled cane.

There are Four Imperial Ones Halls in many Daoist temples. In places ripe with folk religion, the Longevity Constellation is usually worshipped along with the Happiness Constellation and the Success Constellation. The Happiness Constellation is reputed to be capable of bestowing happiness and offspring on those who worship properly, while the Success Constellation can bestow official rank.

There are many other gods, amongst whom the most important are the following:

1) The Great Gods of the Three Realms, also named the Great Gods of the Three Elements. They originated from worship of the sky, earth and water in early times. It was deemed that nothing in the universe could survive without these three basic elements, which the Three Gods personify. Annual festivals celebrating the Three Elements Gods have evolved into the Triplet Days, namely, Superior Principles Day on Day 15, 1st Moon for the Heavenly Element God; Medium Principles Day on Day 15, 7th Moon for the Earth Element God; Lower Principles Day on Day 15, 10th Moon for the Water Element God. Daoism assumed these liturgies. The Five Bushels Sect used to cure followers with letters to the Three Element Gods, on which the patient's name, as well as his or her complaints and confessions were written in three copies. One copy was placed on the mountain addressed to the Heavenly Element God, one copy buried in the earth addressed to the Earth Element God, and one sunk under water given to the Water Element God. People pray to the Three Element Gods for protection. It is believed that the Heavenly Element God descends to the mundane world on Superior Principles Day

to bestow happiness; the Earth Element God descends on Medium Principles Day to warn against crimes; the Water Element God descends on Lower Principles Day to exorcise evil spirits. The Three Elements Gods are commonly worshipped because of their close relationship with daily blessings and curses. There are Three Elements God Halls in most Daoist temples. A lot of communities even designate special temples for the worship of these deities.

◎ The Mother of the Big Dipper.

2) Mother of the Big Dipper. In Chinese her name is Doumu. Dou means Big Dipper, Mu means mother. Therefore she is a goddess who is the mother of all stars of the Big Dipper. She

originally was the imperial concubine of King Yu of the Zhou Dynasty, and was named Madam Ziguang (which means "purple glow"). One spring day when strolling through her garden she suddenly felt as if she had been impregnated. Soon thereafter she gave birth to nine sons. The eldest and the second eldest sons are the Gouchen and Ziwei Emperors (two of the Four Imperial Ones); the other seven sons are the seven stars of Big Dipper. The seven stars control people's time of birth including year, month, day, and hour. As long as they obey the orders of these gods, people will be protected from the stars and lead a safe and smooth life.

Doumu's three eyes represent the heavenly, earthly and human realms; her four heads represent the four Lunar Mansions: the Green Dragon in the East, the White Tiger in the West, the Red Phoenix in the South, and the Black Turtle-Snake in the North; her eight arms represent eight directions. The Sun and the Moon on her hands symbolize heaven and earth, and the bell, the wind, the bow, the rainbow, the gold stamp, the thunder, the spear, the meteor, and the two hands with clutching fingers stand for all the stars surrounding the central Big Dipper.

She is also a very popular Daoist deity. There are Doumu Halls in most Daoist temples.

3) Gods of the Sexagenarian Cycle. The Sexagenarian Cycle was originally a Chinese method of measuring time. The cycle was formed by the interaction of two tables, called the Ten Heavenly Stems (Jia, Yi, Bing, Ding, Wu, Ji, Geng, Xin, Ren, Kui) and the Twelve Earthly Branches (Zi, Chou, Yin, Mao, Chen, Si, Wu, Wei, Shen, You, Xu, Hai). The Chinese paired Heavenly Stems with Earthly Branches, ending up with sixty pairings and used them to calculate time in years. According to Daoist theology, every number or year is presided over by a particular god, called the Year God. Therefore altogether there are sixty Year Gods. Year Gods protect people who are born in the year of their domain, so every person has his or her protecting god. However, if a person commits a foul act, his or her Year God will report it to the Heavenly Court, Thus whenever one's Year arrives, one must be extremely careful in words and deeds. People often buy a red waist belt from a Daoist temple to stay especially attuned to their behavior, so as to have a peaceful year.

There are many versions of the names of the Sexagenarian Gods. The records of Daoist scriptures are different from those on the name tablets in the Sexagenarian Hall at White Cloud Temple in Beijing. Whatever their names may be, they are almost certainly historical figures who performed meritorious deeds.

4) God of Literati. The Chinese name Wenchang was originally the general name for the constellation of the six stars above the first star of the Big Dipper. Ancient astrologers said that this constellation could confer high status upon people, so it became a popular god controlling exploits, fame, and ranks in society. This worship eventually was absorbed into Daoism. Its common name is Wenquxing, which means "the Twisted Constellation of Literature". Around the sixth century Chinese feudalistic dynasties established the System of Imperial Examinations to select officials. Imperial Examinations had become the major passage to an official career. Sacrifice to the Constellation God of Literati grew more and more important, and more and more common. Temples were built all over

◎ Ming Dynasty (Wanli Era) bronze statue of the Literati God (White Cloud Temple, Beijing).

the country in honor of him. He was given the imperial name of the "Emperor of Literati". Annual celebration liturgies were held for him by local governors on the third day of the second moon in the ancient Chinese calendar.

It is said that in Daoism, the God of Literati was named Zhang Yazi. He was a filial son in Zitong County, Sichuan Province during the Jin Dynasty (265-420). He was deified in his hometown after he made great sacrifices on the battlefield as a commander. Around the 13th century, a Daoist wrote a book called *The Biography of Qinghe*, using a particular method of writing in which the author channels a god, in this case the God of Literati. The biography of Qinghe reveals that Zhang Yazi himself was originally a man of the Zhou Dynasty (10th century BCE). The Zhang Yazi born in Sichuan was actually the 73rd incarnation of this man. The Jade Emperor assigned him the duty of presiding over the Cabinet of Literati, which is specifically responsible for the promotion of civilians. Thus Zhang Yazi was regarded as the incarnation of the Literati God. The Yazi Shrine in Zitong County was gradually elevated to become the Palace of the Literati God, and was the founding temple of hundreds of Literati God Temples across the country. In Daoist temples, the image of the Literati God is similar to that of emperors. In many tales, he rides a white donkey, and consorts with two boys, one of whom is a deaf person, named the Heavenly Deaf One; and the other is dumb, named the Earthly Mute. The reason he is aided by the deaf and mute boy is that the affairs he dominates are highly secret, and not allowed to be given away. The one who can speak cannot hear, while the one who can hear cannot speak, so no one can ascertain the secrets of these affairs.

5) The Five Element Emperors are five celestial gods representing the five directions: the Green Emperor in the East, the White Emperor in the West, the Red Emperor in the South, the Black Emperor in the North, and the Yellow Emperor in the Center. They are part of early religion inherited by Daoism. According to Daoism, the Five Element Emperors were primordial. When the universe split into heaven and earth, they transformed into five elements. They represent the five planets in the sky, guiding the celestial gods; the five sacred mountains on earth, ruling the earth gods; the five internal organs in the human body, commanding the gods of the body. They have their own images as well: the Green Dragon in the East, the White Tiger in the west, the Red Phoenix in the South, the Black Turtle-Snake in the North, and the Yellow Emperor in the Middle. The

entire world consists of Five Elements, Five Directions and Five Sacred Mountains. Therefore the Altar of Earth in Beijing, now located in Zhongshan Park, was composed of green, red, white, black and yellow clay during the Qing Dynasty. It was the royal temple where sacrifices were offered to the Gods of the Earth. Its altar symbolizes the entire land of the country. Perhaps because the meanings of the Five Element Gods were too various to give each a certain name, there are four to seven names for each god.

6) God of War. In Chinese his name is Xuanwu or Zhenwu, literally meaning "Dark General" or "Perfect General", because he is the God of the Northern Lunar Mansions, the Black God of the North among the Five Element Gods. His status was not too important until the 14th or 15th century when the Black God of the North grew gradually prosperous, and was endowed with control over exorcisms, blessings, and protections. In 1403, Prince Zhudi of the Ming Dynasty raised a rebellion against his nephew, Emperor Jianwen, and usurped the throne. In order to justify his usurpation with what would appear as the will of higher powers, he had his subordinates fabricate a tale saying that the North God helped him defeat his nephew on the battlefield. After the coronation, he launched large-scale constructions on Mount

◎ Bronze Statue of Emperor Zhenwu from the Ming Dynasty.

Wudang, resulting in many temples dedicated to the God of War, whom he ordered his people to worship. After this time the God of War became a prominent Daoist deity. Many scholars propose that this trend is related to the thirst for protection stirred by repeated invasion from northern nomads at that time. In addition, some scholars found that China's highly developed seafaring technology during the 15th century also enhanced the prosperity of the North God, because north is the direction of water in the Five Elements Theory, and the God of the North is also the God of Water, therefore he is the god of those who depend on the sea. In Foshan City, Guangdong Province, there is still an early temple dedicated to the God of the North where many Chinese living outside of China visit to plea for safe sailing whenever they return home.

According to Daoist scriptures, the God of the North was originally a prince of the Pure Happy Kingdom, but he did not want to succeed to the throne. Instead, he swore to kill all demons in the world, and went to Mount Taihe to cultivate Dao. After he had mastered Dao, he was sent by the Jade Emperor to guard the north. The Jade Emperor renamed Mount Taihe as Mount Wudang, which means "no one can undertake this post except Zhenwu". He usually takes the image of a man with long, flowing hair, wearing black armor and clothing, stepping on a turtle-snake statue with bare feet.

7) Gods of the Five Sacred Mountains. These are gods that Daoism has taken over from early nature worship. According to ancient books in China, as a character for mountain, yue was originally the title for the officials in charge of mountains. Much later, the mountains took the name of their managers. Among numerous worships of mountains, only those of the Five Sacred Mountains were molded according to the five elements theory. People believed that because there are five planets in the sky, there are also five mountains. The descriptions of the Five Sacred Mountains as the immortal lands also shaped the concept of the Five Sacred Mountains.

Before religious Daoism came into being, the First Emperor (Qin Emperor) had been to Mount Tai in 219 BCE to offer sacrifices to Heaven and Earth. Han Dynasty Emperor Wu, escorted by a large band of followers, had first visited Mount Song and Mount Hua , and then went to Mount Tai and Mount Heaven's Pillar in 110 BC for the same purpose. Emperor Wu had given an imperial edict to confirm Mount Tai as the Eastern Sacred Mountain, Mount Heaven's Pillar the Southern Sacred Mountain (later replaced by Mount Heng in Hunan), Mount Hua the Western Sacred Mountain, Mount Heng the Northern Sacred Mountain and Mount Song the Central Sacred Mountain; this edict also prescribed the sacrificial systems and liturgies for these mountains. These mountains from that time on were granted superior status to all other mountains.

Having gradually matured from generation to generation, the sacrificial liturgies for the Five Sacred Mountains were imperial celebrations. Since ancient times, the Five Sacred Mountains have been Daoist paradises of retreat and cultivation.

Concerning the Gods of Sacred Mountains, they were laurelled as Kings during the Tang Dynasty (beginning in the 7th Century). According to *Compilation of Important Books in the Daoist Canon*, the God of the Eastern Sacred Mountain

◎ The Chunyang Hall of the Southern Sacred Mountain.

was honored as King of the Heavenly Navel (here "navel" represents the center of heaven), the God of the Southern Sacred Mountain as King of Heavenly Management, the God of the Western Sacred Mountain as King of the Gold Heaven, the God of the Northern Sacred Mountain as King of Heavenly Safety, the God of the Central Sacred Mountain as King of Central Heaven. They all command thousands of immortal officials and fairy maidens, and watch over their domain. They were elevated to the status of Emperors during the Song Dynasty (12th century). The Emperor of the Eastern Sacred Mountain is dressed in a plain green robe, rides a green dragon, commands 5900 subordinate deities, and determines human birth and death. All persons who have recently died must receive his judgment. He is the commander-in-chief of all ghosts. He has a daughter, named Princess Azure Clouds, who is benevolent and the goddess one prays to when hoping for offspring.

The King of the Southern Sacred Mountain wears a plain red robe, rides a red dragon, and commands 7700 immortals. The King of the Western Sacred Mountain wears a plain white robe, rides a white dragon, and commands 4100 attendants and maids. The King of the Northern Sacred Mountain wears a plain black robe, rides a black dragon, and commands 7000 attendants and maids. The King of the Central Sacred Mountain wears a plain yellow robe, rides a yellow dragon, and commands 30,000 attendants and maids.

8) Gods of Walls and Moats arose from ancient worshipping practices inherited by Daoism. These gods spread throughout China after the 15th century, almost every town having a god of its own. They are all known historical figures, some meritorious officials or generals, some famous doctors or virtuous persons. Their role is to oversee and guard the lives of those in their realm

and to report to the Heavenly Court on a regular basis in order to ensure that humans are keeping their side of the balance of yin and yang in harmony.

9) Gods of Villages. They also developed from land worship. Before Gods of Towns dominated in China, land worship had a hierarchy of deities conforming

◎ The God of Wall and Moat.

strictly to social structure, in which the emperor, kings, dukes, officials and common people were allowed to worship only the land gods within their command; the highest land deity was the Earthly Queen of the Four Imperial Ones. Ranked lower than Town Gods, the Gods of Villages have been very popular among villagers as the grassroot deities since the 14th century during the Ming Dynasty. Some scholars speculate that this change came

© Village Gods.

due to royal edict, because it is reported that the first emperor of the Ming Dynasty was born in a Village God shrine.

The image of the Village God is that of a simply clothed, smiling, white-bearded man. His wife, the Grandma of the Village, looks like any old lady who might live next door.

10) God of the Kitchen. Concerning the God's origin, there are two points of view: one is that it came from the ancient worship of fire, so the God of Fire, Zhurong, and the discoverer of the utilization of fire, Emperor Yan (Yan means hot), are together regarded as the God of the Kitchen. The other is that it used to be a sacrifice to memorialize ancient female cooks. Daoism adopted the latter one by naming the God of the Kitchen as Old Lady of Kunlun and Old Lady of the Fire Seed. There are

five Kitchen Gods, one in each direction: the Eastern Green Kitchen God, the Southern Red Kitchen God, the Western White Kitchen God, the Northern Black Kitchen God and the Yellow Central Kitchen God. In later history, the Kitchen God's functions extended to become protector of the whole family in which she resides, and the messenger sent by the Jade Emperor to every family who reports the good and evil of the family members. The dates of reporting vary from place to place, as do certain customs. There are different rituals when the Reporting Day comes, such as burning the statue of the Kitchen God on the 23rd Day of the 12th Moon, symbolizing sending the Kitchen

◎ The Guandi Hall of the Great Purity Palace in Shenyang.

© The God of Wealth.

God to heaven, and re-inaugurating a new one to welcome him back on the 30th Day of the same month. Many people also paste the statue's mouth with sweet glutinous rice to ask him to report more praises than rebukes; people may also eat candy to express the same meaning.

11) The Gods of Wealth are also household deities who control fortune and success. There are Military Wealth Gods, such as Zhao Xuantan and Guandi, and Civilian Wealth Gods, such as Bigan and Fanli. "Civilian" or "military" labels the secular professions these historical figures used to perform, but has nothing to do with their divine functions.

The most popular Wealth God is Zhao Xuantan, also known as Zhao Gongming, or Marshal Zhaogong. It is reported that he

Daoism in China ·

88

used to be a ghost general subordinate to the Jade Emperor, and a god of plague; afterwards he was subdued by Celestial Master Zhang and was laurelled as Zhengyi Esoteric Altar Marshal because of his effective aid in guarding Zhang's elixir stove. It is reported that he is dressed in a black robe with black armor, rides a fierce black tiger, holds a steel whip, as well as balls that can pacify the sea, and can be used as weapons. Zhao Xuantan also carries a dragon-binding cable. What is especially important is that he commands four aides who help people with business endeavors.

Guandi, or Emperor Guan, originally named Guanyu, used to be a general in the Shu State during the Three Kingdoms Period. He is worshipped as the God of Military Wealth because when he stayed in Caocao's camp, Caocao would make offerings of gold to Guandi whenever he mounted or dismounted his horse. However Guandi did not keep the gold when he departed camp; his loyalty serves as a model of "making money by following the principles of Dao". Today he is still seen everywhere from businesses to household shrines.

Bigan was the uncle of King Zhou, the last emperor of the Shang Dynasty. He is righteous and upright. Displeased by his nephew's atrocities, he spoke out against him. His nephew punished him by cutting out his heart. But people later believed that Bigan cut out his own heart, and put it in front of the King. Yet he did not die, instead swaggering out of the court to hand out money to the masses. He became the God of Wealth among people, because selfless and impartial, he has no heart of his own. It was believed that if a businessman fixed his scale to cheat his customers, Bigan would rebalance the scale to protect the people. He is the symbol of good business morality.

Fanli was a minister of the Yue State during the Spring and Autumn and Warring States Period. It is said that after he abdicated his position, he concealed his true identity, retreating to the state of Qi (now Shandong) to practice business. He was very capable in financial matters, having made a fortune three times, each time distributing the money to the poor. He was called Old Man of Porcelain and Pearl; perhaps he was in these two businesses. He is a model businessman.

12) Divine General Wang is the Guardian God of Daoism. Named Wangshan, he was a historical figure during the reign of Emperor Huizong of the Song Dynasty. He was originally a safeguard of the Jade Emperor's Sacred Heaven Palace, was appointed by the Jade Emperor to be the Town God of Huaiyin

Prefecture in Jiangsu Province. One day, when Perfected Man Sa passed by the temple of Wang, the local governor drove him away under the request of Wang. Sa was shamed and furious, and burnt Wang's temple using magic, making Wang homeless. Wang had no choice but to follow Sa for more than 10 years as a subordinate. During the Yongle era

◎ Wooden statue of Divine General Wang.

(1403-1425) of the Ming Dynasty, a Daoist from Hangzhou claimed to be capable of Wang's mystic techniques of divination. He was so well known that everyone in Beijing heard of him and Emperor Yongle summoned him for consultation time and again. The emperor ordered a temple built for Sa and Wang separately, to the west of the Forbidden City. Whenever he went out for a battle, the emperor would take a cane statue of Wang with him. In the Xuande era (1426 − 1436) of the Ming, Wang was royally laurelled as the Perfect Master of Great Favor, and his shrine was enlarged and renamed as Great Favor Hall. In the Chenghua era (1464 – 1488) of the Ming, the Fire Virtue Temple, home to Wang's hall, was Sacred Attestation Palace. There were annual celebrations on the emperor's birthday, the Lunar New Year, the Winter Solstice, days memorializing his famous predictions, and on occasions when ministers were sent to offer sacrifices. Since then, Wangshan has become the Guardian God in the first hall of Daoist temples, and has been honored as Divine General Wang.

Divine General Wang has a red face with a long beard and three eyes; he wears a red robe with gold armor, and stands on the wheel of wind and fire with finger charms in his left hand and a steel whip in his right. He is upright: he never falls for flatterers, hates evil like an enemy, and supervises all good and evil deeds on both heaven and earth. So there is a saying: "Three eyes penetrate all things under heaven, one whip rouses every person in the world."

CHAPTER 5
DAOIST TEMPLES AND SACRED PLACES

1. The Development of Daoist Temples and their Management Systems

Daoist temples are where Daoists institute their deities, hold mass liturgies and live. The earliest Daoist groups did not have temples. For quite a long time after Zhang Daoling founded his sect, the places of activity were political centers, meditation rooms and communal hostels. Political centers were the offices of Daoist officials and also their meeting centers in what were, at the time, small theocracies Meditation rooms were places where followers came to be cured, meditate and communicate with deities. Communal hostels were places where local communities

◎ The Guest Room of the Celestial Master Mansion in Jiangxi Province.

accommodated pilgrims and descended deities.

Nowadays Daoist temples are called guan (which originally meant a watchtower on either side of a gate), gong (palace), tai (terrace), dong (cave, but also can mean "insight"), an (hut), tang (hall), yuan (yard), or miao (temple). It is said that immortals dwell on tai or in guan, which were originally made of gold and white jade. What is considered to be the earliest Daoist temple, Louguantai, in Zhouzhi County, Shaanxi Province, was originally the astronomical observatory of Yinxi, one of Laozi's disciples and a local governor of the Zhou Dynasty, so its name comprised Lou (storied building), Guan and Tai. It was the place where

Laozi wrote and first taught the *Daode Jing*. In the last half of the 2nd century BCE, Emperor Wu of the Han Dynasty believed in immortal doctrines. When he learned that immortals liked to reside in high buildings, he ordered the construction of Feilian Guan in the capital of Changan (now Xi'an), and Yanshou Guan in the suburbs, to amuse immortals. It was the first time Guan was used in the name of a Daoist temple.Emperor Wu of the Northern Zhou Dynasty (561-582) ordered all Daoist temples to assume guan as their names. During the Tang Dynasty (after the 7th century), the royal families claimed Laozi as their ancestor. After that time, all temples in honor of Laozi were renamed as

◎ The Eternal Happiness Palace (Ruicheng County, Shanxi Province).

palaces. In later centuries, as more and more immortals were praised and conceived of as emperors, more and more temples became called palaces. "Gongguan" has become the general name for Daoist temples.

The architectural styles of Daoist temples has varied with times, environment and deities until the 13th century when the overall arrangements of all Daoist temples were converging. Most medium to large-sized Daoist temples roughly consist of a gate, bell tower, drum tower, Divine General Wang's Hall, Central Hall, Jade Emperor Hall, Three Pure Ones Hall, and sect founder hall. Many temples also have preserved relics of historical figures.

All temples established a united administrative system: every temple had a well-trained, saint-like abbot, aided by a dean to oversee all administration. Daoist officials were divided into the following categories: liaison officials, hall managers, preachers, treasurers, cooks, warehouse managers, disciplinary officials and dormitory managers. Some large temples had several assistants for each section. There were strict disciplines for each official's position, and any violation would be punished.

After the establishment of the People's Republic of China in 1949, all temples have done away with feudal management, and assumed democratic management. Temples are administrated by a Democratic Management Committee whose members are produced through regular elections. Committee members, through group discussion, decide all important affairs. Some temples also set up modern institutions such as a receptionist office, administrative office and an office of security, but the basic temple functions have not changed. Though Zhengyi Daoism masters have families and homes, they usually live very close to their temples, where nearly all religious activity occurs. They are part of the temple's democratic administration and obey its principles.

2. The Sacred Places of Daoism

There are more than 4500 Daoist temples in Mainland China. Most of them are not only the places of daily religious activity, but also important cultural sites and tourist attractions. Among them the most important ones are the following:

1) The Five Sacred Mountains of Daoism. Mount Tai is the paramount Sacred Mountain. It is located among the counties of Tai'an, Licheng, and Changqing in Shandong. The altitude of the highest peak is 1545 meters. The worship of Mount Tai originated in the 20th century BCE during the Xia Dynasty. Emperors of all past dynasties went there to offer sacrifices. The Temple of Mount Tai, located at the foot of the mountain, is the central temple for the God of the East. The whole compound occupies 98,000 square meters. The central hall is 22.3 meters high, 48.7 meters long, and 19.8 meters wide, covered with yellow glaze tiles, giving it the flavor of a palace. There is a large-scale fresco on its inner walls, 3.3 meters tale and 63 meters long,

◎ Morning sunshine on Azure Cloud Temple (Mount Tai).

depicting the scene of an inspection tour of the Eastern God, escorted by more than six hundred people. It is reported to be a work of the 12th century, with great artistic and cultural value.

Azure Cloud Temple is located on top of Mount Tai, which enshrines the princess of the Eastern God. It is a building dating to the Song Dynasty. The ridge of the roof, like the beak of some great bird, as well as the eave bells of the central hall are made of bronze, while the tiles on the halls of the wings are made of iron. There are two bronze steles built in the 15th century in the courtyard. Other Daoist buildings are Queen Mother's Hall, Mother of the Big Dipper Hall, Ascending Hall and Jade Emperor Hall.

The Southern Sacred Mountain, Mount Heng, is in

Hengshan County, Hunan Province. There are 72 peaks among which the highest is Zhurong Peak (1290 meters). It is famous for its beautiful natural scenery, and is recognized as the most elegant sacred mountain in China. It has been a Daoist Sacred Mountain since ancient times. It is said that Laozi once came to Mount Heng, bestowed the better part of the *Daode Jing* onto King Zhurong, and taught him how to rule under the guidance of Dao. The Queen Mother also came here to teach Madam Wei how to cultivate in the Jin Dynasty. It is recorded that 109 famous Daoists cultivated at Mount Heng since the Han Dynasty, among whom 9 succeeded in achieving Dao. King Zhurong himself is also the God of the Southern Sacred Mountain. The Temple of the Southern God is at the foot of Mount Heng, construction of which began in the Tang Dynasty and experienced countless repairs and enlargements in past dynasties. The existent building was re-constructed in 1882 during the Late Qing Dynasty. The whole compound occupies 98,500 square meters, in which the central building is 22 meters high with 72 pillars symbolizing the 72 peaks of Mount Heng. The outer buildings include the Sleeping Palace, the Royal Study and the Winding Dragon Pavilion. In 1997, the Daoist Association of the Southern Sacred Mountain reconstructed Chunyang's Hall, Benevolent Longevity

Hall, Master Lao's Hall, the Jade Emperor's Hall and the Medicine King's Hall, adding 7900 square meters to this compound, making it a magnificent building with an ancient style.

Other Daoist buildings on the Southern Sacred Mountain are Xuandu Temple on the middle of the mountainside, Founder Master's Temple at Heaven's Southern Gate, and Yellow Court Temple at the foot of Sages' Meeting Peak. Most of these buildings were destroyed by long wars before 1949 and during the Cultural Revolution (1966 – 1976). They were rebuilt and even enlarged during the 1980s under the efforts of the local Daoist association. The Yellow Court Temple is said to be the last cultivation place of Madam Wei, in front of which there is a giant rock,

◎ The Eastern Yard of Jade Spring Monastery (Mount Hua).

said to be her spot of ascension.

The Western Sacred Mountain, Mount Hua is in the South of Huayin County. In Chinese "hua" means flower. It is named Flower Mountain because the five peaks together make it look like a lotus. The altitude of the highest peaks is around 2200 meters. It has always been famous for its steep slopes, and is recognized as the most dangerous sacred mountain in China. There have been many famous Daoists who cultivated in this mountain, leaving numerous relics such as Xiyuan (Western Element) Cave, Huashan Cave, Lotus Cave, Jade Emperor's Cave, Supreme Cave, Congratulating Longevity Cave, Greeting Sunrise Cave and Xiyi's Cave. The Temple of the Western God is at the eastern end of the town at the mountain base. Construction began during the reign of Emperor Wu of the Han Dynasty (140-89 CE), and reconstruction projects began in 576 during the Northern Zhou Dynasty, in 836 during the Tang Dynasty and in 961 during the Northern Song. The existing buildings are the results of recent reconstruction in the Ming and Qing Dynasties. The grand central hall was a palace that accommodated visiting emperors. The steles in the courtyard, valuable cultural relics, are authentic records of this temple's history.

The Jade Spring Monastery is at the mouth of the northern

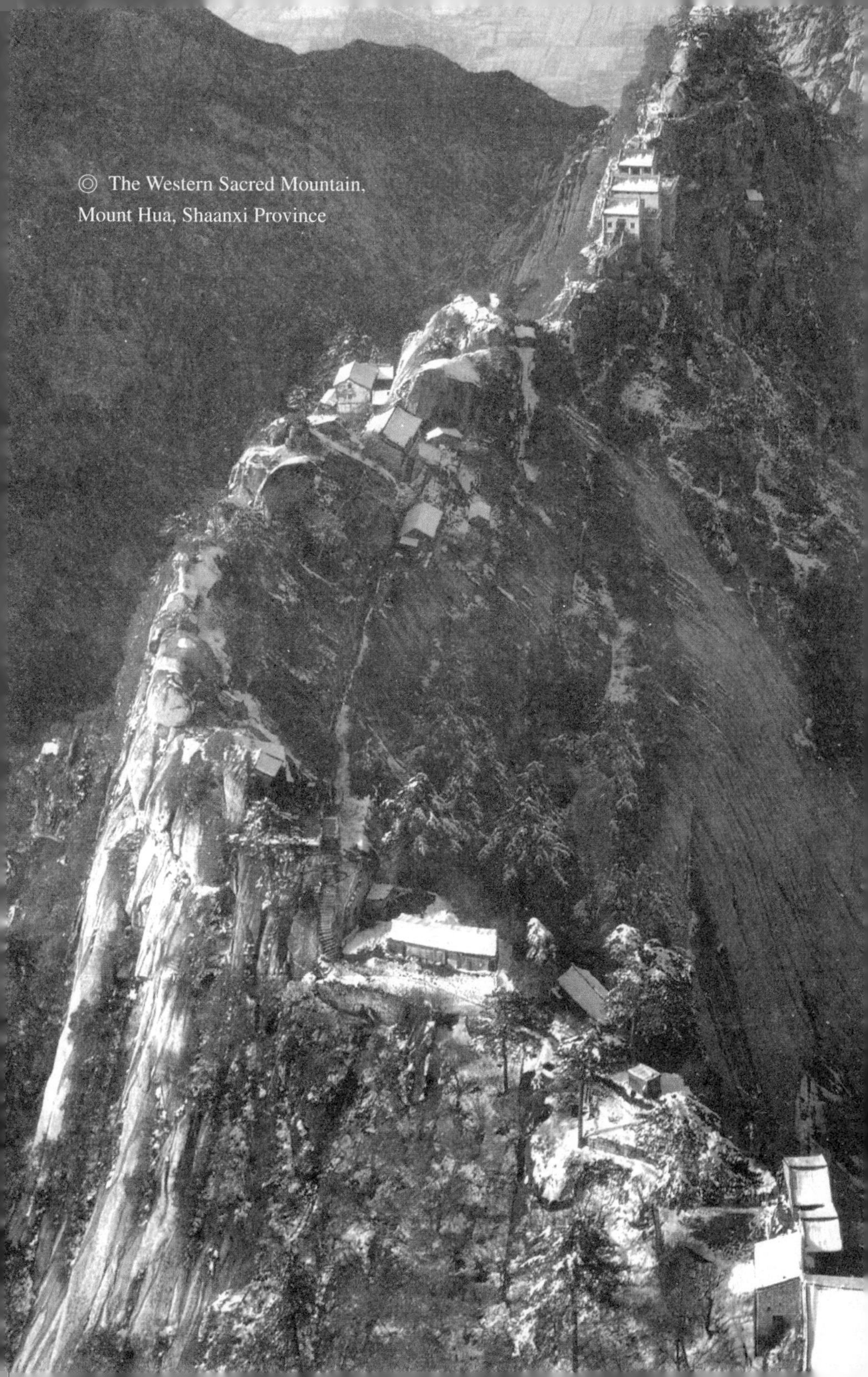

◎ The Western Sacred Mountain,
Mount Hua, Shaanxi Province

valley. It is recorded that Chentuan, the famous Daoist monk of the Song Dynasty, cultivated there. After his ascencion, his disciples built Xiyi Shrine as the memorial (Xiyi is the honorific of Chentuan, and means "diffuse" and "remote"). After several enlargements during the Qing Dynasty, it was renamed Jade Spring Monastery. In the 1980s, the Daoist Association of Mount Hua added the newly built cloister and rock garden to the delicate ancient compound. This temple compound has been arranged in three sections. The middle section highlights Xiyi Shrine; the eastern section contains Huatuo's Tomb (Huatuo was a famous doctor of the Three Kingdoms period), cloister and the Twelve Caves; the western section contains the stone boat and Xiyi's Cave. The eastern yard is the only passage to the mountain. It used to be a private school during the Ming Dynasty before Daoists transformed it into a place for religious practice in 1714 during the Qing Dynasty; therefore the place is quite small. The major hall consists of only three rooms, within which the Black Lady of the Empyrean is enshrined.

Mountain Guard's Palace, also called Upper Palace, is located in the valley between Jade Maiden Peak, Lotus Peak and Goose Perching Peak. Enshrined with the God of the West. There is a well in the yard, which is believed to lead to the Jade Spring

Monastery.

Emerald Cloud Palace is on the top of Lotus Peak. It is the temple of the Third Holy Mother and her son, Chenxiang. There is a giant rock beside the temple, with a crevice in it, and it looks as if it were cut apart by a huge axe. It comes from a legend about Chenxiang saving his mother. According to the story, the goddess in the temple was a Heavenly fairy maiden, but she could not bear the loneliness. So she descended to the mundane world, married without permission and gave birth to Chenxiang. Her second eldest brother who was a general of the Jade Emperor was sent

◎ The beautiful scenery of the Southern Sacred Mountain.

down to capture her and placed the giant rock on her, trapping her. Having grown large, Chenxiang split the giant rock and freed his mother.

The Northern Sacred Mountain Mount Heng is in Hunyuan County, Shanxi Province. The altitude of the highest peak is 2017 meters. The Northern Sacred Mountain was originally Mount Damao in Quyang County, Hebei Province. In 1403, when Ming Dynasty Emperor Chengzhu moved the capital from Nanjing to Beijing, he thought it was unreasonable to worship Mount Damao as the Northern Sacred Mountain, because it is to the south of Beijing. He ordered the Northern Sacred Mountain transferred from Mount Damao to Mount Heng. However, it was not convenient to offer sacrifices to Mount Heng because the transportation to Hunyuan was difficult and northern tribes often roamed the area around Hunyuan. Thus liturgies were still held at Mount Damao to offer sacrifices indirectly to Mount Heng. It was possible for memorial sacrifices to be held in Hunyuan until Emperor Shunzhi's reign during the Qing Dynasty. Up to now the large central hall of the original Northern God's Temple built in the Yuan Dynasty remains in tact, which is the largest existing building from the Yuan Dynasty. The huge frescos on the four walls were the Yuan Dynasty artists' imitations of the Tang

◎ The Northern Sacred Mountain, Mount Heng,　Shanxi Province.

painter, Wu Daozi. Mountain worshipping activities began as early as the Zhou Dynasty. There were already many cultivators dwelling in the mountain during the Han Dynasty. In the 7th century, during the Tang Dynasty, Daoism on Mount Heng was quite prosperous. Most of the existent Daoist buildings were constructed during the Ming Dynasty.

God Heng Hall, also called Primordial Spirit Palace, is the temple of the Northern God, alongside his four ministers and four marshals. It was constructed in 1501 during the Ming Dynasty. Other attached buildings include a temple library and a bell-drum tower. There are also more than ten steles in the yard, among them an iron stele erected in 1324 during the Yuan Dynasty.

North-west of God Heng's Hall is Gathering Immortals Hall, in which the Three Constellations of Happiness, Success and Longevity and other immortals from various celestial ministries are enshrined. To the east of God Heng Hall is Jade Emperor Pavilion and Royal Stele Pavilion. Construction of Sleeping Palace began on the Supreme Peace Terrace during the reign of the Great Wu Emperor of the Northern Wei Dynasty (424 – 452), which used to be the central hall of the Northern God Temple. The existent building was constructed in the Ming Dynasty, and is dedicated to the Northern God and his queen.

The Central Sacred Mountain, Mount Song, is in Dengfeng County, Henan Province. The altitude of the highest peak is 1440 meters. It has been the object of mountain worship since ancient times. It is reported that in 110 BCE when Emperor Wu of the Han Dynasty was on the mountain, he heard the forest winds and thought they sounded like hails of "Long Live the Emperor!" He was so delighted that he issued bans on cutting trees and grass, ordained it as a sacred mountain, and renamed it "Long Live Mountain", and built upon it its summit, Long Live Pavilion, and at its base, Long Live Watch. This is why the laudatory shouting for emperor was called "shanhu" (mountain shouting). Empress Wu Zetian of the Tang Dynasty mounted and consecrated this mountain twice in 688 and 696. It is she who renamed the county as Dengfeng, which means climb and consecrate.

◎ Yaocan Pavilion and Middle Heavenly Tower of the Central Sacred Mountain Temple, Henan Province.

In current times, as most of the mountain temples have been converted to Buddhism, the Central God Temple at the mountain's eastern foot is the major Daoist temple. It has been built, repaired, rebuilt and expanded throughout past dynasties. It was repaired nine times during the Qing Dynasty alone. The present monastic compound spreads more than 110,000 square meters, embracing more than 300 halls and pavilions, as well as a library and a dormitory. As the central building, Junji (Extremely Craggy) Hall was rebuilt in 1653 during the Qing Dynasty, partially destroyed by Japanese air raids, and then restored after 1949. The inner statue of the Central God is 5 meters high. In the yard there are more than 330 ancient cypress trees from the Han, Tang and Song Dynasties, and more than ten ancient steles. The especially valuable and rare Daoist relics are the four iron titans standing in front of the Chongsheng gate.

2) The Three Founder Temples of the Quanzhen Sect: White Cloud Temple in Beijing (outside Xibianmen), and Eternal

◎ The gate of the White Cloud Temple in Beijing.

Happiness Palace and Double Yang Palace, both in Shaanxi.

White Cloud Temple was initiated as Tianchang Temple for Laozi in 739 of the Tang Dynasty, and rebuilt as Taiji Palace in 1203 during the Jin Dynasty. In 1224, when the founder of Dragon Gate Sect, a sub-sect of Quanzhen, came back to Beijing from the long journey to meet with Genghis Khan, he resided at Taiji Palace. Since he was honored as "Eternal-Spring Perfect Man" by the Khan, his temple was renamed as Ever-Spring Palace. He stayed in the temple for three years for missionary work before he passed away and was buried under the Pliable Residence Hall. Hence Eternal-Spring Palace has become one of the founder temples of the Quanzhen Denomination. It was destroyed by flames of war at the end of the Yuan Dynasty and rebuilt during the Ming Dynasty. In 1443 of the Ming Dynasty, Emperor Yingzong bestowed the temple with a tablet inscribed on which is its new name, White Cloud Temple, the name still used today. White Cloud Temple was very prosperous during the Qing Dynasty. The famous Abbot Wang Changyue held ordination assemblies there three times, in which he converted and ordained more than 1000 Daoist monks. When Emperor Kangxi was a prince he visited White Cloud Temple to be proselytized. Therefore its acreage increased greatly. Now it occupies more

◎ Wooden statue of Founder Master Lu (Lu Dongbin) from the Ming Dynasty.

than 60,000 square meters, and contains more than 10,000 square meters of buildings, including the Halls of the Divine General, Big Dipper's Mother, Three Elements Gods, Wealth Gods, Jade Emperor, Three Pure Ones, Four Imperial Ones and some other items such as Blocking Wind Bridge [1], Bell and Drum Tower, Commandment-Receiving Platform, and a garden. At present it is the working place of the China Taoist Association (CTA) and the China Daoist College, founded in 1957 and 1991, respectively.

Eternal Happinese Palace, formally named Chunyang Palace of Longevity, is in Ruicheng County, Shaanxi Province, the birthplace of Lu Dongbin. Chunyang, meaning Pure Yang, is Lu Dongbin's Daoist name. After Lu passed away, the people of his

[1] White Cloud Temple used to have a Buddhist temple, named Qingfeng Si (Gentle Breeze Temple) to its south. At the time, the two religions were fiercely competing, and Daoists did not want the "bad winds" of the Buddhist temple to enter White Cloud Temple, so they constructed a bridge to keep the winds out.

hometown rebuilt his family house into Lu's Shrine. Having been expanded into a Daoist monastery under the order of a Yuan emperor, it was named after the town as "Eternal Happiness", or "Yongle". It is one of the founding temples of the Quanzhen Sect. In 1959, while the Sanmen Gorge Dam was being constructed, this temple was moved to present day Longquan Village. The major buildings include Dragon Tiger Hall, Three Pure Ones Hall, Chunyang Hall, and Chongyang Hall, all of which are Yuan Dynasty constructions. The most famous relics are the frescos on the walls, which are masterpieces of Chinese

◎ A portion of the fresco at Eternal Happiness Palace.

art. Taking 120 years to complete, they cover 960 square meters. *The Pilgrimage to the Origin* fresco in the Three Pure Ones Hall is 94.68 meters long and 4.26 meters high, and contains 286 figures. It vividly depicts a scene of numerous immortals making their pilgrimmage to visit the Heavenly Sage of Preexistence. It was praised as "The Crown of Eastern Art". Now it is on the list of National Cultural Relic Sites.

Chongyang Palace, formally named Chongyang Palace of Longevity (often abbreviated as "Founder's Temple"), is at Liu-Jiang Village, Hu County, Shaanxi Province. It was the birthplace of Wang Chongyang. After Wang Chongyang passed away in 1170, his disciple Wang Chuyi took the corpse back to Hu County, and built up a shrine at the site where Wang first cultivated. Afterwards, his disciples begged donations to build up the temple, which is recognized as a founding temple of the Quanzhen sect. At the zenith of its expansion during the Yuan Dynasty it contained 5000 rooms. Now this compound has shrunk to less than 8,000 square meters. Most of the buildings such as Master Lao's Hall and Founder's Hall were reconstructed during the Ming and Qing Dynasties. However there are still more than 30 steles dating back to the Yuan Dynasty, inscribed in both Chinese and Mongolian, precious relics of Daoist history.

◎ Laozi Hall at Louguantai in Shaanxi Province. There is a stele of the *Daode Jing* in the yard whose characters resemble plum flowers.

3) The Earliest Daoist Temple. Louguantai is at the foot of Mount Zhongnan in Zhouzhi County, Shaanxi Province. It is said that it was initiated in the 10th century BCE during the Zhou Dynasty. It used to be the astrological observatory of Yinxi, called Caoloutai, which means Thatched Pavilion Terrace. Yinxi was a local official of the Zhou Dynasty. When he observed purple clouds coming from the east, he was sure that a great sage was on the way. He therefore abandoned his official position and went to wait at Hangu Pass. Laozi arrived on a black ox. Laozi was

invited into the thatched tower, and instructed Yinxi with the *Daode Jing* and other skills. Thereby Louguantai was also called Sermon Terrace. The First Emperor of Qin was entranced with theories of immortality as well as with Laozi; he had a temple built to the south of the tower, called Pure Temple. Emperor Wu of Han added a temple to the north side of the tower, called Expecting Immortal Palace. In the Tang and Song Dynasties, emperors who fervently believed in Daoism had Louguantai expanded into a huge monastery, considered at the time one of the best Daoist centers in China. Famous Daoist masters flocked there, among whom included a greatly revered master of the Quanzhen sect, Lu Dongbin. Lu cultivated and achieved Dao at Louguantai. Tang emperors regarded themselves as the descendents of Laozi, crowned Louguantai as the Ancestor Sage Palace, which means it is the temple of the royal ancestor. They even assigned lands to the temple as they would to royal relatives. This story was recorded on the remnant stele inscribed by Ou Yangxiu, a great scholar of the Tang. Another existent stele tells the story of the close relationship between the Tang court and Louguantai: one night in 741, Emperor Xuanzong dreamed of Laozi. A jade statue was excavated from the spot on the southeastern hill indicated by the dream. A temple named Meeting

God Temple was ordered to be built on the hill, which was subsequently renamed Sacred Presence Hill. A Song Emperor renamed Ancestor Sage Temple as Heaven-Abiding Empire-Reviving Temple, and lauded Laozi as Supreme Emperor of the Primordial Chaos. There are two steles from the Song Dynasty by the famous calligrapher, Mifei, and the great scholar, Su Dongpo. However Louguantai has been destroyed and rebuilt repeatedly since the Yuan Dynasty. The important extant buildings are Laozi Temple, Divine General Hall, Mother of the Big Dipper Hall, the library, Sermon Terrace and Laozi's Tomb.

4) The Birthplace of the Supreme Pure Sect. Mount Mao lies across the four counties of Jurong, Jintan, Lishui, and Liyang. The mountain was

◎ Three-Heaven Gate on Mount Mao.

◎ A temple on Mount Mao.

originally named Mount Juqu. It is recorded that three brothers, Maoying, Maogu and Maozhong came here to cultivate in 82 BCE during the reign of Emperor Zhao of the Han Dynasty. They cured people with herbs. After they transcended the world, in order to memorialize them, the local people renamed the mountain as Mount Mao and named the three highest peaks as Mount Mao One, Two, and Three. Hereafter Mount Mao has always been one of the great retreats of Daoists, many of whose fame spread wide. During the Jin Dynasty Gehong cultivated and composed his great work, *The Master Who Embraces Simplicity* at Mount Mao; in 364, Xumi, Xusun (son of Xumi) and Yangxi founded the Shangqing Sect there; in 488, a famous

Daoist theorist, Tao Hongjin, composed *Instruction of Truth and Catalogue of the Daoist Pantheon* at Mount Mao.

Many buildings have been built there since the Tang Dynasty, making Mount Mao one of the three centers of Zheng Yi Daoism. Daoists on Mount Mao received countless favors from past emperors. For instance, all forests and lands that used to be public were designated as the territory of the temple. After the 16th century, Quanzhen Daoists began to establish temples on the mountain as well, making it a sacred mountain shared by the two Daoist Denominations. In the 1930s, when the Japanese invaded Eastern China, Mount Mao became a base of the Chinese Communist New Fourth Army. Daoists on the mountain actively joined the resistance, and some of them joined the Communist Army. The Daoists on Mount Mao have made great contributions whilst suffering great losses. All temples on the mountain were burnt by Japanese invaders and many Daoists were brutally killed. In 1949, Daoists from all temples on the mountain organized an administrative group and began to rebuild temples. In 1963, the construction of Roof Palace along with its statues was completed on the highest peaks. A consecration ceremony was held that year.

Daoist Activities were forced to cease during the Cultural

Revolution. It was not until the 1980s that Daoist organizations were re-established and some important Daoist buildings and relics were rebuilt under government aid. Roof Palace, formally named The Highest Sky Complete Happiness Palace, was constantly restored from 1982 to 1998. Its major buildings include Divine General Hall, the Library, Great Original Jewel Hall, Holy Parents Hall, Three Heaven Gate, and Ascendance Terrace. Great Original Jewel Hall is the central hall, within which are enshrined the Perfect Masters, along with the Three Maos, with carved stone busts of 45 deities and the memorial tablets of famous Daoists from the past who cultivated on Mount Mao. Holy Parents Hall was dedicated to the parents of the Three Maos. It is said Gehong used the ancient well in the yard to mix elixirs.

Original Tally Palace is said to be the cultivation place of Tao Hongjin. It was constructed as a temple in the 8th century. Emperor Huizong of the Song dynasty renamed it *Original* Tally Palace, and granted it a Jade Seal; therefore it was also called Seal Palace. Most of the extant buildings were rebuilt in 1988, including Observatory Gate, Divine General Palace, Stele Pavilion, Longevity Terrace, and Great Origin Jewel Palace. Observatory Gate used to be the astrological working place of Daoists. It is a 21.8 meter-wide and 7.5 meter-high stone building with three gates, which were restored in 1987. Longevity Terrace used to be the "Holy Terrace" on which specially designed liturgies were regularly held to pray for emperors and queens' blessings during the Song and Yuan Dynasties. The three-tiered blue stone terrace was restored in 1992. A stone boat was placed at the center of the top level. In the 1990s, the Daoist Association of Mount Mao built up a 33-meter statue of Laozi on the adjacent slope. It has become a symbolic cultural sight of Mount Mao.

Heavenly Origin Temple is said to be the elixir-mixing place of occult master, Li Mingzhen, of the Qin Dynasty. In the 11th century (during the Yuan Dynasty) it was expanded into a Quanzhen monastery. In 1993, it was

◎ Jianfu Temple on Mount Qingcheng.

◎ Permanent Dao Temple on Mount Qingcheng.

rebuilt into a Quanzhen nunnery with several halls, in which the important relics are the Elixir Well of Perfect Man, Li Mingzhen, and the Tomb of Kang Youwei's Mother (Kong Youwei was a famous modern Chinese politician and scholar).

5) The Birthplace of Religious Daoism. Located at the eastern end of the Qionglai Mountain Range, Mount Qingcheng, which means Green City Mountain, is in the southwest of Dujiang Weir County, Sichuan Province. With heavy forests and thirty-six peaks, it is recognized as the most serene sacred mountain in

China. It used to be named Ghost City Mountain because the primitive residents believed in ghosts, however it was named Du Mountain during the Qin and Han Dynasty. In 221 BCE, when the Qin Emperor united China, he ordered royal sacrifices to the 18 sacred mountains, among which he listed Du Mountain. As Governor of Shu Prefecture (under the Qin Dynasty), Libin and his son initiated and presided over the construction of the world-renowned irrigation works, Dujiang Weir, in the late Warring States period. Because Mount Qingcheng is the central area where Zhang Daoling founded his Daoist sect, early Daoist liturgy was greatly influenced by customs of local minority tribes. Being the cradle of religious Daoism, all past generations of Celestial Masters and numerous other Daoists made pilgrimages to Mount Qingcheng.

The extant important structures on the mountain include Celestial Master Cave, Founder Master Hall, Supreme Pure Palace, Constructing Happiness Palace, Round Bright Palace, and Pure Jade Palace. Celestial Master's Cave, also known as Permanent Dao Temple, is located on the 1,000 meter sloped terrace between White Cloud Brook and Crabapple Brook. It is a compound of 7200 square meters with halls of the Three Pure Ones, the Yellow Emperor and the Three August Ones. There is actually a cave inside the Celestial Master Hall, from which the temple derives its name. It is a cave in which Zhang Daoling lived, and within which is an enshrined stone statue of his image from the Sui Dynasty. It is a place all past Celestial Masters were required to visit. Founder Master Hall was dedicated to the famous Daoist Priest, Du Guangting, of the Tang Dynasty, who studied and composed here, as well as Zhang Sanfeng of the Ming Dynasty, a legendary master of cultivation and martial arts. The famous general, Feng Yuxiang, lived in this hall during World War II, and left a stele in memory of the victory.

Shangqing Palace lies to the south of the terrace; the construction on the Palace began in the Jin Dynasty and it was rebuilt most recently in 1869 (Qing Dynasty). The temple's tablet is inscribed with the calligraphy of former president of the Nationalist Party, Jiang Jieshi (Chiang Kaishek). There are halls of the Three Pure Ones, the Jade Emperor, Confucius-Guandi, and the Eastern God. The Yin-Yang Wells in the yard are twin wells, one of which is square, shallow and turbid, the other round, deep and clear. Numerous paintings and works of calligraphy by the modern artist Zhang Daqian (Chang Dai-chien) are preserved in this temple.

Master Lao's Pavilion on the highest peak is a recent

construction, with excellent views of the mountain scenery.

6) The Central Sacred Site for Emperor Zhenwu. Mount Wudang, also known as Great Harmony Mountain, lies in Jun County, Hubei Province. With 72 peaks, 24 ravines, 11 caves, 9 springs, 9 wells and a 1612 meter crowning peak, the mountain's mystical beauty has long inspired myth and legend. Long before religious Daoism was founded, Mount Wudang had been peopled with occult masters. After religious Daoism was formed, it entered the popular imagination of Daoists. It is from this mountain that Yinxi, Lu Dongbin, Sun Simiao, Chentuan and Zhang Sanfeng have poured fresh brooks into the spiritual waters of Daoist history. It is said that Emperor Zhenwu cultivated in the mountain for 42 years and then transcended the worldly realm. Since the 11th century, legends and books about him have spread throughout the country, making Mount Wudang the central site of the North God, also called the God of Water, Emperor Zhen Wu, or the God of War. However this god's functions were not confined to the aforementioned. He is also God of Fertility, God of Fortune, and even more important, is another embodiment of Taiji, directly related to Dao, and is therefore especially revered by alchemists.

Daoists on Mount Wudang have fused Confucianism and Buddhism with Daoism, upheld loyalty and filial piety, and practiced martial arts as part of health cultivation. The fame of its Daoist inner martial arts are parallel to Shaolin Temple's

◎ The Great Harmony Palace of Mount Wudang.

Buddhist outer martial arts. Daoist inner martial arts, such as Taiji Quan (Shadow Boxing), Bagua Quan (Eight-Diagram Boxing) and Wudang Sword Fighting, put Daoist theories of "overcoming the hard with the soft and controlling the moving with the still", into practice, advocating the principles of "taking defense as purpose, attacking only when threatened, and relying completely on inner energy."

Initiated in the 7th century during the Tang Dynasty, Daoist buildings on Mount Wudang have been destroyed and repaired repeatedly during past dynasties. In 1412, Emperor Zhudi of the Ming Dynasty hosted the largest scale construction on Mount Wudang in order to repay the grace that the North God had obliged him. It took 8 years to complete the 8 palaces, 2 temples, 36 shrines and 72 caves. Since then it has been the center of Emperor Zhenwu's worship. These buildings have been badly damaged by wars and disturbances in the past 100 years, especially during the 1920s. In March 1931, troops of the Red Army under Marshal Helong quartered at Mount Wudang, and received aid from local Daoists, many of whom were cruelly suppressed by the Nationalist Party after the Red Army departed. Many Daoist leaders were killed.

The extant Daoist temples include Great Harmony Palace, Purple Sky Palace, Gold Roof, Recover the Perfect Temple, and South Cliff Palace. Purple Sky Palace at the foot of Unfolded Flag Peak, which was initiated in 1413, is the largest temple on the mountain and the working place of the Mount Wudang Daoist Association. The buildings of the temple align in three rows of which the eastern one is the East Palace, the western one is the West Palace and the middle one contains the Halls of Dragon-

Tiger, Ten-Direction, Purple Sky and Parents. Dragon-Tiger Hall enshrines the Dragon and Tiger Protector. Ten-Direction Hall enshrines the Divine General, along with a 9 meter high, 90 ton stele inscribed with the tale of Emperor Zhudi's rebuilding of Mount Wudang. Purple Sky Hall, which was constructed on a platform, is the central hall, which enshrines Emperor Zhenwu. There are 33 statues of the Emperor, among which the central and largest one resembles an emperor's; the four medium-sized bronze statues on either side depicting youth, as well as middle and old age; the smaller 28 statues are on the eastern and western walls. In Parents Hall, the first floor enshrines the Holy Parents of the Emperor, while the second floor enshrines the Jade Emperor and the Mother of the Big Dipper.

Great Harmony Palace was established in 1416. The central hall enshrines a golden statue of the Emperor, along with the Eight Heavenly Masters of the Thunder Ministry on either side. Other buildings include Worship Hall, Bell-Drum Tower, Chanting Hall, Three-Element Gods Hall, and a theater. On the opposite peak, Little Lotus Peak, is a small house called Transferred Hall. It acquired its name because there is placed on it a miniature bronze temple-house on a stone altar which was donated by followers from Hubei, Henan and Zhejiang in 1307

(Yuan Dynasty); it was transferred from Golden Roof according to the order of Emperer Zhudi, who thought it too small to be on the highest peak.

The Gold Roof is the top of Heaven's Pillar Peak, the mountain's tallest peak. On top of it is an all bronze hall built upon a granite terrace. It is 5.54 meters high, 4.4 meters long and 3.15 meters wide, and was constructed in 1416 using 21 tons of bronze and 30 kilograms of gold. The inner statues of the Emperor, Divine Generals of Water and Fire, and male and female escorts, as well as all the houseware were also made of gold-plated bronze. The place shines golden indeed!

Some other sacred Daoist sites are too important to be ignored. They are the Temple of the Wall and Moat in Shanghai, Three Elements Palace in Guangzhou, Mount Luofu in Guangdong, Mount Lu in Jiangxi, Great Pure Palace in Shenyang, Obscure Mystery Temple in Suzhou, Master Lao's Cave in Chongqing, Mount Lao in Qingdao, Mount Qian in Liaoning, Black Goat Palace in Chengdu, Eight Immortals Palace in Xi'an, and Mount Mian in Shanxi. All of them are storehouses of Chinese history and culture. Their mystic beauty continues to draw those who seek history, peace and unity with nature.

CHAPTER 6
IMPORTANT DAOIST SCRIPTURES AND THE COMPILATION OF THE DAOIST CANON

1. The Development of Daoist Scriptures

Daoist scriptures are numerous because Daoism has adopted many various ancient thoughts and beliefs. The most important contents comprise work concerning immortal doctrines and treatises on yin-yang, the five elements, astrology, medicine, numerology, Logicianism, Moism, military strategy and Legalism in the Spring and Autumn and Warring States Period. There also existed many "celestial books" or "sacred books" on millenarianism which spread among the masses in the 2nd century during the early stages of religious Daoism, as well as books written by followers and scholars corresponding to the demands of feudal society, and receiving Confucian and Buddhist influence in later times. The subjects range from history to philosophy to ethics, astronomy, medicine, metallurgy, aesthetics, theology, anthropology, cultivation of the body, charms, liturgies, and commandments. The extant Daoist Canon of Scriptures, compiled during the reigns of the two emperors, Zhengtong and Wanli, of the Ming Dynasty, has 5485 scrolls in total, making it the only religious canon that can compare with the Buddhist Tripitaka.

Similar to Daoist religious development, the canonization and compilation of Daoist books have experienced a long historical process. In the 2nd century, the books that were canonized by the Five Bushels Sect and the Supreme Peace Sect were *The Book of Supreme Peace*, *Daode Jing* and its commentaries, such as Xiang'er and Heshanggong's commentaries. Since its first appearance, *The Book of Supreme Peace* had many different names and versions. *The Daode Jing* has been the most important book canonized and explained by Daoist founders, descendents and followers from varying perspectives. Among the commentators still available today, Heshanggong's (which means "The Revered Old Man by the River"), was the first to explain the *Daode Jing* from the perspective of Huang-Lao Daoism. This commentary, which is commonly regarded as a work edited during the middle of the Eastern Han Dynasty, formulated the theory of Identification Between Body and State, which proposed that the principles of cultivation of health and state management are identical in that both require purity, reduction of desire, and wuwei.

Daoist scriptures increased with the development and spread of Daoism. In the Eastern Jin Dynasty when Gehong wrote *The Master Who Embraces Simplicity*, he listed a catalogue with 1299 scrolls worth of Daoist books in his Further Reading Chapter. With the rapid spread of the Zhengyi Sect, Daoist charms and liturgies had been further theorized, resulting in the production of many Daoist classics. These works come from three major traditions: Shangqing, Lingbao and Sanhuang. The Shangqing tradition honored Madam Wei, who ascended on the Southern Sacred Mountain, as its founder. Its representatives, among who are Yangxi and Xumi, composed many works in Madam Wei's name. The most important one is the *Shanqing Insight into the True Classics*. The Lingbao tradition claimed that its earliest scripture had been found in a stone city by Helu, King of the State of Wu during the Warring States Period. The Supreme Master Lao had sent Three Sage-Perfect Men to grant many scriptures to Gexuan who had cultivated at Tiantai

Mountain. The Lingbao continued to amass scriptures as well. The Sanhuang tradition honored Baoliang, father-in-law of Gehong, as its founder. There are different stories in Daoist books concerning the origin of these scriptures: one is that they were found in a stone house on the middle sacred mountain by Baoliang in 292 AD; the other is that they were granted to Baoliang by Baoliang's teacher, Zuo Yuanfang, or Zhengying, an occult practitioner of the Eastern Han Dynasty. The majority of the contents of the Sanhuang scriptures are about exorcist rituals, charms, talismans and cultivation methods of concentration on deities. All scriptures of these three traditions converged into *The Daoist Canon of Scriptures*.

2. Compilations of the Daoist Canon

The compilation of the Daoist Canon started in the Tang Dynasty, when Daoism had its first prosperous period. Under the support of Emperor Li's royalties, the collection and compilation of Daoist scriptures reached new heights. Tang Emperor Xuanzong ordered Shi Chongxuan and forty other scholars to compile *The Complete Daoist Scriptures* during his Kaiyuan era (713-741 AD), and this work reached 113 scrolls in sum. Using this work as a base, he sent researchers into provinces to bring back Daoist texts. These were then compiled into the first Daoist Canon, the *Exquisite Compendium of Three Insights*. "Insight" is a translation of the Chinese, Dong, which many western scholars translate as "grottoes", because the basic meaning of dong is "cave" or "grotto". However, here it is related to "tong", which means "communicate". Sandong are actually three ways of communicating with deities, in other words, three insights into the supernatural. These texts are all believed to be revelations from deities. The total number of scrolls recorded was 3744, which were classified according to their contents into three canons with 36 subdivisions: Insights into the Perfect, with 12 subdivisions; Insights into the Mysterious, with 12 subdivisions; Insights into the Sacred, with 12 subdivisions. It was named *The Daoist Canon of Kaiyuan* because it was printed in the Kaiyuan era.

The Song Dynasty is the second period in which Daoism was exalted. Daoist Canons were compiled on six occasions during the Song: 1) In the early years of the Song Dynasty, Emperor Taizong ordered officials of all local governments to search for Daoist books. More than 7000 scrolls were collected. After making many amendments, duplicates were erased. This compilation reached 3737 scrolls. 2) In 1008 AD, further supplement reached 4359 total scrolls. 3) In 1012 AD, this work was supplemented to become *The Precious Canon of the Celestial Palace of the Great Song* containing 4565 scrolls. 4) For the convenience of the emperor's reading, the chief editor Zhang Junfang extracted 122 scrolls from more than 700 of the most important classics in the *Daoist Canon of the Great Song* to compile *Yunji Qiqian* (literally translated as *Cloud Chests with Seven Labels*, meaning a complete Daoist Canon), popularly called *The Small Daoist Canon*. 5) Emperor Song

◎ Ming Dynasty woodblock-printed Daoist Canon (White Cloud Temple, Beijing).

Huizong believed firmly in Daoism. During his reign, the Daoist Canon was re-compiled twice; the later edition was *The Daoist Canon of Wanshou*, which contained 5481 scrolls. 6) In 1179 AD during the Southern Song Dynasty, compilation was once again launched by royalty to rebuild the Canon scattered in warring Northern China; they ended up with the same number of scrolls as in the *Wanshou Canon*.

In the meantime, Emperor Zhangzong of the Jin Dynasty, who ruled Northern China, ordered Daoists to supplement the *Wanshou Canon*. The fruit of their efforts was *The Precious*

Xuandu Canon of Great Jin (Xuandu is the name of a Daoist temple), which reached 6455 scrolls. The new edition of the *Xuandu Canon*, compiled in 1244 during the Yuan Dynasty, contained 7800 scrolls and was supplemented with scriptures of the Quanzhen sect which was rising at that time.

These editions of the Daoist Canon have mostly been lost; only a few remnant scrolls survive. The available editions today are the *Zhentong Daoist Canon* and *Wanli Supplementary Daoist Canon*. These are fruits of projects undertaken under the Ming rulers, Yingzong in the 15th century and Shenzong in the 17th century. The total volume of the two editions reached 5485 scrolls.

The scriptures were arranged in *Three Insights* or *Three Primary Canons*, *Four Secondary Canons* and *Twelve Accessory Canons*. The so-called *Three Insights* or *Three Primary Canons* followed the classification of past editions. All scriptures believed to be granted by the Heavenly Sage of Preexistence (Yuanshi Tianzun) were classified as Insights into the Perfect, of which most were from the Lingbao tradition; all scriptures that were believed to be bestowed by the Supreme Master of Dao (Heavenly Sage of the Lingbao) were classified as *Insights into the Mysterious*, of which most were from

◎ Photo-printed Daoist Canon of the early years of the Republic of China, preserved in White Cloud Temple, Beijing.

the Lingbao tradition; all scriptures that were believed to be granted by the Supreme Master of Lao were classified as *Insights into the Sacred*, of which most were from the Sanhuang tradition. The so-called *Four Secondary Canons* include the Great Purity, Great Peace, Great Mystery and Zhengyi canons. All books in these canons were expository and complementary to the *Three Insights*. Great Purity Canons were expository and complementary to *Insights into the Perfect*; Great Peace to the Mysterious; Great Mystery to the Sacred; and Zhengyi to all Three Insights. *The Twelve Accessory Canons* contained scriptures which could not be classified into *The Three Insights* or *The Four Secondaries*. *The Twelve Accessory Canons* were: *Texts*, *Sacred Talismans*, *Jade Secrets*, *Sacred Charts*, *Theogonies*, *Commandments*, *Liturgies*, *Cultivation Methods*, *Esoteric Skills*, *Biographies*, *Hymns* and *Sacred Memorials*.

In 1900, when the Eight-Power Allied Forces invaded Beijing, the printing boards of the Zhentong Daoist Canon and the Wanli Supplementary Daoist Canon were burnt. Only one set of Daoist Canons of the Ming was preserved well at White Cloud Temple. From 1923 to 1936, in order to rescue this cultural heritage, Zhao Erxun, along with many famous scholars initiated reprints. They took the Daoist Canon of White Cloud Temple as the source copy and had Hanfenlou Bookstore in Shanghai reprint 350 copies. There are 1120 volumes in one set. These copies were called Hanfenlou's Version, which is the major version of the Daoist Canon today. The common classics such as *Daode*

Jing, *Zhuangzi*, *Book of Divine Deliverance*, *Classic of Pure Quiet*, and *Book of the Intuitive Enlightenment*, all are included in this collection.

There was no new edition of the Daoist Canon produced in Qing Dynasty, but some reference books were edited, such as *Compilation of Important Books in the Daoist Canon*, *The Contents of the Compilation of Important Books in the Daoist Canon*, *Basic Index of Compilation of Important Books in the Daoist Canon*. The earliest edition of *Compilation of Important Books in the Daoist Canon* was completed by abstracting 173 books from *The Daoist Canon of the Ming Dynasty* during the Jiaqing era (1796-1820). Through gradual supplementation, this collection increased to 287 books in 1906. Other than the original 173 books, all of the 114 books which were supplemented later were not included in *The Daoist Canon of the Ming Dynasty*. Hence they became important materials for the study of Daoism during the Ming and Qing Dynasties.

Another important event of the Qing Dynasty was the discovery of ancient scrolls by a Daoist monk named Wang Yuanlu in the 17th Cave at Dunhuang at the beginning of the 20th century. Some long-lost Daoist classics were found among these scrolls, which are called the *Dunhuang Daoist Scriptures*. These books concern 496 items, are hand-written, and date from the 6th to the 10th century, mostly from the period during the reigns of Tang Gaozong and Tang Xuanzong. Most of them are fragmentary, yet they remain important relics of very high historical value for Daoist studies. They are very important in supplementing the *Daoist Canon of the Ming Dynasty*. As a result of political corruption during the Qing Dynasty, these scrolls were stolen from China, first by a British man named Aurel Stein in 1907, subsequently by a Frenchman, Paul Pelliot, then by a Russian, Pyotr Koslov, and a Japanese, Zuicho Tachibana. After the establishment of the People's Republic of China, with the joint efforts of the Chinese government and overseas friends, a small number of the scrolls have been brought back to their homeland and preserved there.

3. Compilations of the Daoist Canon after 1949

After the establishment of the People's Republic of China in 1949, and especially since the implementation of reform policies in the 1980s, independence and prosperity have brought about a national cultural flourishing. In 1981, the World Religions Institute of the Chinese Academy of Social Sciences began to organize scholars to compile *Synopses of the Daoist Canon*, which was published in 1991. Chief-edited by Ren Jiyu, a famous scholar of religious studies in contemporary China, this book included all entries of the 1473 books in the Daoist Canon. Using the structure of the *Imperial Collection of Four*, it researched the books' author and time period, introduced the contents in every entry, and wrote *Resumes of Authors and Editors*, *A New Classification Directory*, *Contents of the Daoist Canon and its Supplements*, and *An Index of Authors and Titles*. It is a good reference book for Daoist Canon studies. In 1988, in order to satisfy the study of Chinese history, culture, philosophy, religion, medicine and health care,

State Cultural Relic Publishing House, Shanghai Bookstore and Tianjin Ancient Work Publishing House photo-printed the Daoist Canon of the Ming Dynasty again, every set of which has 36 volumes.

In the 1990s, Bashu Publishing House in Sichuan invited some Daoist scholars to compile *Daoist Books Outside the Canon*. This compilation collected hundreds of Daoist books outside *The Daoist Canon of the Ming Dynasty*. The 26 volume collection was not arranged according to the classification of the *Ming Canon*. Instead, the books were classified into ten groups according to content: the lost ancient Daoist books, classics, tenets and decrees, cultivation of health, commandments, liturgies, biographies of immortals, records of temples and sacred places, literature and catalogues, and addendums. It reflected the modern development of Daoism, and facilitated Daoist studies. The dates of the composition of the selected books were recorded as before the establishment of the People's Republic of China

All of the books consist of three parts: 1) Books that were prior to but not collected in *The Daoist Canon of the Ming Dynasty*, such as the Huang-Lao Daoist silk scrolls excavated at Mawangdui in Hunan in the 1970s, which are few but quite valuable; 2) Different versions of some books already collected in *The Daoist Canon of the Ming Dynasty*, which are important for comparison; 3) books that are posterior to *The Daoist Canon of the Ming Dynasty*, which are manifold in this compilation. All books except Mawangdui silk scrolls were photo-printed, retaining their original appearance, enabling readers to glimpse rare or even unique copies, as well as private copies. The range of the collection was extensive, including some books by non-Daoists. This not only enriched the contents of the Daoist Canon, but also mirrors the Daoist tendency towards secularization, as well as the unification of the three major traditional Chinese ideologies. Some Confucianists were wild about Daoist studies and cultivation, and wrote many works on these subjects. Thus arose many writings concerning the differences among the three ideologies. Consequently the publication of *Daoist Books Outside the Canon*, was welcomed warmly by both Daoists as well as Daoist studies circles home and abroad.

In August 1996, the China Taoist Association, the World Religions Institute of the Chinese Academy of Social Sciences and Huaxia Publishing House jointly set up a Compilation Committee for rectification, edition and publication of the *Chinese Daoist Canon*. This project had been placed among the Important Programs of the Ninth and Tenth Five-Year Plan of the National Publication Project. This edition of the Daoist Canon covered all books from the Ming edition and the most important Daoist books outside the Ming edition; all collected books were arranged according to four basic categories: primary scriptures, secondary scriptures, commandments, and Daoist history. All texts were emended, punctuated, typed, composed, and printed with modern techniques and scholastic standards. All 49 volumes of this collection were published in 2003.

CHAPTER 7
THE CHINA TAOIST ASSOCIATION

Since the 15th and 16th century, China's traditional schools of Confucianism, Buddhism, and Daoism have fused more and more deeply. In the beginning of its history, Daoism followed two general trends: one was the pursuit of longevity by emperors, nobles and scholars; the other was the activities of folk cults. Although many important Daoist thinkers have *Daoists of the Ming and Qing Dynasties much, including the compilation of classics, the development of inner alchemical techniques, and the expansion of Daoist theology.However* , the social influence of Daoist organizations has tailed off in recent times. For example, Mount Emei in Sichuan and Mount Heng in Hunan used to be Daoist Sacred Mountains, occupied by Daoist temples, but have been overtaken by Buddhist ones. In the 19th century, China had been reduced to a semi-colonial and semi-feudal country Daoism,

147

along with Chinese culture, were devastated. Most Daoist temples were destroyed by war and chaos; Daoist organizations were short of social and financial support, and slowly withered; most Daoist clerics were poorly educated, being unable to study their own tradition. However, the social and cultural foundation of Daoism has been preserved in traditional culture and folk custom.

1. The Establishment of CTA and its Early Events

Since 1949 when the People's Republic of China was established, the Chinese Communist Party and Chinese government have implemented a policy of religious freedom. The Constitution of China clearly stipulates that citizens have the freedom to believe or not believe in religions, that the difference of religious belief should not bring about any difference of right or obligation, and that all religions are legally equal.

Although Daoism has less clerics and temples than any other religion, it has the same right of religious freedom, and is protected by the law. In 1956, after Buddhism and Islamism first set up their national associations, some notable Daoists proposed a China Taoist Association (abbreviated as CTA), and Daoists throughout China responded to such a proposal. In April 1956, the First National Conference of Daoist Representatives was held in Beijing. At that time they declared the establishment of CTA, elected the Council of CTA that was composed of members from both the Zhengyi and Quanzhen Denominations, among whom

◎ White Cloud Temple in Beijing-The Founding Temple of the Dragon Gate Sect and the Working Palace of CTA.

Yue Chongdai, the Abbot of the Supreme Pure Palace (Taiqing Gong) in Shenyang and the 26th generation Liturgy Master of the Dragon Gate Sect, was appointed to be president. They decided the working place would be White Cloud Temple in Beijing.

CTA is the first national cross-denominational organization in Daoist history. Its current institutions, which are responsible for coordination of Daoist affairs, include the Ecclesiastic Affairs Office, Liaison Office, Office of Research, and Administrative Office.

The activities of CTA were forced to cease during the Cultural Revolution (1966 — 1976). Since the end of that period, the CTA has continued to hold its National Representative Conference every five years, and its Standing Council has held elections six times. In addition, there are now more than fifty local Daoist Associations in China.

In the 1950s and 1960s, the biggest challenge for Daoism in China was to restore and revive its poor state. CTA organized the repair of damaged temples and the collection of scriptures under government support. It also mobilized Daoists to study culture, politics and religious teachings. The second President and famous Daoist scholar, Chen Yingning, chaired the drafting of *The Working Plan*

◎ The Library of Qinchiyang Temple in the New District of Pudong, Shanghai.

151

Concerning Daoist Research and the Intellectual Training of Clerics, and decided to have Daoists and scholars collect and compile Daoist books, rubbings, papers and pictures in order to write a *History of Chinese Daoism*. The detailed *Synopses of the Daoist Canon* exceeds 300,000 Chinese characters; they completed the first edition of *Memorabilia of Daoism in Past Dynasties* and final editions of several books, among which *A Brief Introduction to Daoism* was the first systemic introduction to Daoism in modern times. They also issued the only Daoist magazine, *China Taoism*.

Concerning clerical training, CTA initiated Chinese Daoist Clerical Training Classes in September, 1962. There were two kinds of Daoist training programs: Senior Training, with the goal of training Daoist researchers, and Clerical Training, meant to educate the administrative and liturgical staff. The curricula is composed of three main categories: (1) the basic Daoist subjects, which include tenets, denominational history, major classics, commandments, and liturgy, (2) basic cultural knowledge, which includes the history of Daoism, autobiography of Daoist historical figures, the philosophy of Laozi, Zhuangzi and other schools, and (3) the Daoist cultivation subjects, which include qigong, medicine, as well as inner and outer alchemy. The length of training is five years. The graduates from the classes numbered more than thirty persons, all of who have become the cadre staff of Daoism throughout China. These classes were forced to cease during the Cultural Revolution.

2. The Events of Daoism in the Era of Chinese Reformation

Since the 1980s, Chinese Daoism has been becoming prosperous with the rapid development of the economy and society, as well as policies of religious freedom.

First of all, CTA has played a role as mediator between the government and Daoists.

After having re-commenced work for a few years, CTA held the Third National Representative Conference, which modified its constitution, and elected a new council and president in May, 1980. It took more than ten years to rectify the mistaken religious policies of the Cultural Revolution, establish just ones, redress mishandled cases, and return and repair the occupied or closed temples.

Now temples have been re-opening, undergoing reconstruction and some are even being constructed for first time. Many young people have also been converting to the religion and becoming Daoist monks (see Introduction). However, it is impossible to calculate the common believers of Daoism because there is no formal proselytizing ritual for laypeople. A research published in *Shanghai Daoism* (the 1st issue of 2003) revealed that, among the temple goers of the nine Daoist temples in Shanghai, 32% were male, 68% female; 46% between 30-60 years old, 45% above 60; 50% were primary school graduates, 41% middle school graduates; more than half had believed in Daoism for over 15 years, about one third had believed for 8 to 15 years, and more than one half believed in two religions, mostly in Daoism and Buddhism.

The purposes of individual participation in temple activities were found to be 42% for petitioning for safety, success in one's career, and health, 20% for cultivation, and a very limited percentage for abundant harvest, happy marriage and coming offspring, which mirrors the betterment of living conditions.

The rapid development of this socialist country also encourages the enthusiasm of Daoists. The leaders of Chinese Daoism agree that as the only indigenous Chinese religion, Daoism has unique cultural resources and profound roots in folk culture, and can play a positive role in China and the world. With the implementation of religious freedom policies in China,

◎ The Vice President of CTA, Zhang Jiyu, talking with a British Daoist during the Conference of World Religions and Development, UK.

Daoism can adapt to socialist society, and can play an important part in promoting social stability by guiding people to assume proper living values and cultivate harmonious spiritual states. Daoism can show people how to maintain independent morality and spirituality while sailing in the currents of social development, how to abide by natural rules in maintaining a sustainable harmony between nature and society, how to construct a peaceful world of equality by balancing the world economic development and the common welfare of human beings, how to restrain from greed for extravagance while enjoying basic material satisfaction, and how to cultivate effectively by integrating personal salvation and altruism. It a method that involves both patriotism and piety.

Since 1978, under the coordination and promotion of Daoist associations at all levels, Chinese Daoist temples have done much work for social welfare, such as almsgiving, public donation and tree planting. In 1993, the CTA held the first convention to commend model individuals and groups with respect to both patriotism and religious piety, in which 53 groups and 159 persons received honors. In the summer of 1998, when the Yangtze River, Songhua River and Nen River flooded, the Chinese Daoist Association donated 5,600,000 RBM yuan in disaster relief funds. Daoists have won respect and trust from the people; in 2003 there were five Daoist priests elected as national political

◎ The Daoist Association donating to flood victims, 1998.

consultants and three as national people's representatives, two of whom hold standing membership in both organizations.

Second, the CTA has also reassumed Daoist traditional systems and liturgies that had ceased for tens of years. The CTA has instituted and issued rules concerning temple affairs and Daoist clerics, and facilitated the administration of Daoist affairs.

The Quanzhen and Zhengyi sects have their own specific succession systems and liturgies, of which the Quanzhen's are named chuanjie (literally means "pass down commandments"), and Zhengyi's, shoulu (literally means "bestow the sacred registry"). The system of chuanjie in Quanzhen Daoism, founded by Qiu Chuji in the 13th century, has a history of over 700 years; and that of Shoulu in Zhengyi Daoism, founded by Zhang Daoling in the 2nd century, has a history of over 1800 years. The shoulu assemblies were often held on the days before Triplet Days, because these are occasions when the Three Elements Gods inspect human deeds and determine blessings and curses accordingly.

It subsequently became a custom for the Celestial Masters to ascend on altars and bestow sacred registries in the Mansion on Mount Dragon and Tiger on the Triplet Days. Lu is the registry book of deities from all directions, but also the certificate to summon divine generals to execute Daoist orders. Zhengyi Daoists believe that only after having been bestowed with lu, can they ascend to the Heavenly Court and get divine positions. Only those who have divine positions can make their memorials to Heaven heard or seen in ceremonies, and thereby command divine soldiers or generals.

Shoulu ceremonies are presided over by the Three Masters of Proselytism, Inspection, and Recommendation. Since the 24th generation, the Celestial Master was authorized by Emperor

◎　The Shoulu Rituals of Zhengyi Daoism.

◎ Disciples perform the commandment rites by following the Instructing Master at the first Chuanjie Rituals of the PRC (White Cloud Temple, Beijing, 1989) .

Zhengzong of the Northern Song (reigned from 997 − 1022) to set up a Shoulu Court in the capital city, and in ceremonies, the Proselytizing Master has always been played by the Celestial Masters themselves.

In the Daoist tradition, Chuanjie and Shoulu are not only ordination ceremonies which call for participants' belief in Dao and their commitment to priesthood, but also educational ceremonies to regulate the words and deeds of priests. In modern times, war and chaos made the implementation of this system cease for tens of years. For example, White Cloud Temple in

Beijing is the central place of chuanjie, but there had been no such kind of ceremony since the 1920s.

It was the long desire of Daoists and the demands of the times as well to reassume these rituals of passage. In November 1988, it was decided to hold a chuanjie ceremony in White Cloud Temple on the Second Meeting of the Fourth Session Council of the CTA. On Day 2, Moon 12, 1989, the long absent chuanjie ceremonies were re-initiated at White Cloud Temple in Beijing, and lasted for twenty days. The Chair Master was the 22nd Abbot of White Cloud Temple in Beijing, Wang Lixian; the 17 Auxiliary Masters came from other important Quanzhen temples. There were 45 Quanzhen monks and 30 nuns who participated, among whom the oldest was 75 years old and the youngest, 21 years old.

During these days, drum and bell sounded together in the morning, the participant monks and nuns rose early, dressed in yellow robes, and scriptures in hands, chanted along with presiding masters. This happened three times per day: morning, noon, and afternoon. After the participants were instructed with all important rites and classics, they were bestowed with Primary, Secondary and Celestial Commandments, respectively, along with Commandment Certificates accordingly. These serve as their religious identity cards, certifying what level of rites, commandments, and hence ordination rank they had received.

In November 1995, CTA held the second Chuanjie assembly on Mount Qingcheng in Sichuan. There were 546 Quanzhen monks and 166 nuns from across the country who participated, among who the oldest was 120 years old, and the youngest 21. The president of CTA and the 23rd generation succession master, Fu Yuantian, presided over the ceremonies. What was unique this occasion was that there were several lectures on cultivation methods for nuns, moral practices, and master-student relationships. Some Daoist scholars and artists were also invited to observe the ceremonies.

The third Chuanjie assembly was held on Mount Qian, Liaoning Province in August 2002. About 400 Quanzhen monks and nuns participated in this event, including some from Hong Kong, Taiwan, Malaysia and Singapore. 200 people received complete ordainations and 200 people received partial ordainations.

The situation of Zhengyi priests is quite different from that of Quanzhen clerics in that their lives are more similar to those of common people. Thus the importance of ordination ceremonies to Zhengyi priests is not limited to the priesthood recognition, but to elevate their consciousness of social responsibility for preaching and salvation. CTA made some investigations into Zhengyi priests, held colloquia, and compiled and issued some documents on shoulu.

In October 1991, CTA re-initiated shoulu ceremonies on

◎ Disciples following the rites in the Chuanjie Days at Five Dragon Palace on Mount Qian in Liaoning.

Mount Dragon and Tiger for 36 Zhengyi priests from Taiwan, Singapore and Malaysia.

From September 5th to 7th, 1995, CTA held the first shoulu ceremonies for Zhengyi priests in Mainland China on Mount Dragon and Tiger. More than 190 persons attended the rites, among whom the oldest was 70 years old and the youngest was less than 20. A senior priest from Mount Dragon and Tiger played the role of Proselytizing Master. After performing a series of rites prescribed by traditional regulations, all the participants succeeded in obtaining their divine positions.

On the Lower Principles Day in November 2002, the Celestial Masters' Mansion held master-disciple recognition ceremonies for more than 60 Daoists from Taiwan, Hong Kong, Singapore and Indonesia.

In the meantime, in order to purify and conserve the spiritual tradition of Daoism, reform the confusing situation between Daoism and folk religions, and Daoist clerics and wizards, CTA issued Administrative Measures on Daoist Temples and Trial Measures on the Administration of Zhengyi Priests in 1992.

The former file prescribes that all Daoist temples must establish a Democratic Management Committee through election among the resident clerics. This committee then takes the responsibility for internal affairs. All activities held in any temple must conform to Daoist traditional norms, abide by the constitution and laws of the country, and may not engage in any feudal superstitious activity in the name of Daoism. The financial affairs, cultural relics protection, recruitment, external liasons, and accommodation for visiting clerics must be executed according to regulations.

These policies were issued to protect legal rights and interests of Zhengyi priests, and administrate their activities according to standard rules. It demands that all Zhengyi priests must be patriotic, law-abiding, and religiously proselytized formally to the Three Jewels: Dao, Scriptures and Masters. They must have a master-disciple lineage, be able to recite *The Precious Instructions of the Founder Masters* and *The Classic of Morning and Evening Monastic Lessons*, perform the daily rites of the Zhengyi Denomination, abide by the norms of the words and deeds of a priest, and pass the examination, thereby receiving the recognition of Daoist organizations. CTA uniformly grants Certificate of Daoist Priests to qualified Zhengyi applicants. They must accept the administration of the local Daoist temple or association, and hold ceremonies in registered temples. If they hold a ceremony in a followers' house as local traditional custom requires, they must have the agreement of the local Daoist temple or association, and avoid disturbing the social, living or productive orders.

These policies have played positive roles in promoting the preservation and development of the Daoist tradition.

Thirdly, CTA has founded the first Daoist school in

history to train new generations of Daoist clerics.

Daoism has been passed down through master-disciple lines since it came into being. Although there were some knowledgeable masters who gave special seminars during their spiritual wanderings, these courses were not consistent and the topics were not systematic. After its foundation in 1957, CTA held one Daoist cleric training program in 1962, and six during the 1980s, and had 206 graduates in total, most of whom have become the major functionaries in Daoist temples and associations across the country today.

In May 1990, CTA founded the China Taoist College (CTC) at White Cloud Temple in Beijing on the bases of the former training programs. The tenets of CTC are: to educate young Daoists to have a certain level of Daoist knowledge and accomplishment, to be both

◎ Students of CTC reading the books of the Ming and Qing Dynasties.

patriotic and pious, and to volunteer to serve in the Daoist vocation and carry on and develop Daoist tradition and culture. There are two kinds of classes: specialized classes and general classes. The former are

◎ Nuns in discussion.

two-year classes to train administrators for temples. The applicant should have at least two years of experience as a Daoist cleric, have the recommendation of a local Daoist temple or association and the approval from his or her family. They must also pass an entrance examination. The latter are also two-year classes, for which the applicants are good graduates from the former school or local Daoist schools.

The main courses of the college are Daoist History, Teachings, Liturgies, Commandments, Introduction to Daoist Classics, Daoist Liturgical Music, Catalogue of the Daoist Pantheon, Daoist Cultivation Methods, Daoist Sculpture and Pottery, Temple Management, Foreign Language Study, Calligraphy, Chinese History and Geography, World History and

Geography, and Legal Knowledge. The teachers who host the courses are reputable Daoist masters and famous Daoist scholars. CTC has recruited about 200 students after its foundation. It has become the central place to train middle and high-level Daoist clerics.

Additionally, CTC has hosted some temporary programs. In May 1997, it held a seminar for 27 principals of Daoist temples from 20 provinces, among whom 17 were male and 10 were female, 24 were of the Quanzhen sect, and 3 were of the Zhengyi sect. It held a class for 22 Zhengyi priests in Shanghai from 1998 to 2001, all of whom were qualified graduates from the Shanghai Daoist College.

◎ Lecture at Shanghai Daoist College.

There are some local schools or seminars hosted by Daoist associations of various levels, such as Shanghai, Sichuan, Wuhan, Mount Mao, Suzhou, Shaanxi and Lanzhou. Most of the temples also have systems or programs of training and studies. Thus CTA has formed a pyramid system of Daoist education, with CTC at the summit.

◎ Students of CTC in a computer class.

Fourth, CTA has researched Daoist doctrines and history in order to carry forward Daoist culture.

In May 1980 when CTA resumed work, it made a decision to take studies on Daoism as its key project. By 1986, the Study Office of CTA had published 16 issues of *CTA Journal*, the predecessor to *China Taoism* magazine, which has become a periodical since 1987. Now it is a bimonthly journal issued in

China and abroad and has a distribution of more than 8,000 copies. It is welcomed by readers who want to learn about Daoist history, doctrines, and studies, as well as CTA proceedings. It has the fourth largest overseas circulation among Chinese social science periodicals.

There are also other Daoist magazines issued by some local Daoist associations, such as *Shanghai Daoism*, *Sanqin Daoism and Fujian Daoism*.

CTA has also published some books on Daoism and many Daoist scriptures, accounting for about 1,154,000 copies of more than 120 titles altogether, among which the most important ones are the *Great Dictionary of Daoism*, *Album for Chinese Daoism*, *An Introduction to Daoism*, *Daoism and Health Cultivation*, *Commentary on the Daode Jing*, *Collection of Daoist Calligraphy and Paintings* and *The Classic of Morning and Evening Monastic Lessons*.

In order to promote Daoist studies by ecclesiastic and scholastic groups, both at home and abroad, CTA set up the Daoist Culture Institute (TCI) in 1989, through which CTA has entered a broader field of Daoist studies by compiling books and hosting symposiums.

In autumn 1992, TCI, the Xi'an Daoist Association and Eight

◎ CTA publications.

Immortals Palace in Xi'an jointly hosted the Xi'an Daoist Culture Symposium, which 55 representatives from 12 provinces attended, as well as representatives from Japan and France.

TCI and Mount Wudang Daoist Association jointly held symposiums twice in 1993 and 1994 on Mount Wudang, in which 40 representatives from China, Japan, Italy and Korea participated and more than 30 theses were delivered.

TCI and Immortal's Cave Temple on Mount Lu in Jiangxi Province held symposiums twice in 1998 and 1999, in which more than 100 representatives from Mainland China, Hong Kong and Taiwan participated and more than 100 theses were delivered.

◎ Some overseas Daoist monks from the UK, Germany and Korea in a meeting hosted by CTA.

The themes covered the status of Daoism, its role in Chinese traditional culture, the modern values of Daoism, trends of Daoism in the new century, and the Daoist relationship to socialist construction.

In August 2001, TCI, along with the Daoist association of Jiangsu Province, Mount Mao and Nanjing University, held a symposium on Mount Mao, the theme of which focused on Prospects for Daoism in the 21st Century.

In November 2002, TCI and the Shanghai Daoist Association held joint symposiums in Shanghai, the topic of which was

"Daoist Thought and Social Progress in China", and nearly 100 representatives presented. Reverend Min Zhiting, the President of CTA, stated in his speech that: "In order to carry on and develop Daoist teaching, we must understand that on the one hand, we have entered a new stage of building a generally prosperous society. Therefore Daoist doctrines have to adapt to the progress of a Socialist society, and on the other hand, now that we are in a time of globalization, Daoist doctrines have to adapt to the progress of human civilization." Reverend Zhang Jiyu, the Vice President of CTA, observed that under the new historic condition,

◎ Symposiums on "Daoist Thought and Social Pogress in China" hosted by TCI and the Shanghai Daoist Association, November 2002.

◎ The representative of CTA receiving memorial gifts at the Consecration of Three Pure Ones Hall (Mount Lotus, Malaysia).

all Daoists were very concerned about how to play a more important role in social development. All of the participants agreed that Daoism emphasizes the unification of cultivating Dao and accumulating virtues, and deems that to fulfill social duties is an indispensable part of the doctrine of immortals; the basic tenets of Daoism are unchangeable, while the method of organization, contents of commandments, liturgies and exorcisms alter with the times.

These events have deepened the study and public understanding of Daoism, spread its social influence and produced many constructive proposals.

Fifth, CTA has developed friendship with Daoists in Hong Kong, Taiwan, Macao and foreign countries, and actively participated in world affairs for peace and justice.

The central government of China implements the policy of One China, Two Systems in Hong Kong, Macao and Taiwan, so the religious bodies and individuals in these three Chinese zones do not affiliate with each other, nor do they intervene with each other; instead they have mutual respect for one another. The intercourse between CTA with Hong Kong Daoist circles began formally on the Middle Principles Day of 1985, when 35 Quanzhen Daoists from Zique Daoist Temple in Hong Kong visited White Cloud Temple in Beijing to pay homage to the founding temple, and joined in the celebration ceremony.

In January 1986, Reverend Li Yuhang, President of CTA, went to Mount Luofu in Guangdong Province to

◎ A Daoist delegation from Taiwan during its visit to White Cloud Temple.

◎ The Vice President of the Hong Kong Taoist Association presenting a gift to the Official of the Religious Affairs Bureau during a Hong Kong Daoist Festival.

preside over the re-opening and Abbot inauguration celebration, on which occasion he encountered the Vice President, Wu Yaodong, and Chairman Lu Chongde of the Hong Kong Daoist Association, as well as the Vice Abbot, Zhao Zhendong, and Deng Guocai of the Yuen Yuen Institute in Hong Kong. They had friendly talks, establishing formal links.

In October 1986, a delegation from the Hong Kong Daoist Association visited CTA in Beijing and the Mount Laoshan Daoist Association in Shandong, interviewed Zhao Puchu, the Vice President of the Chinese Consultant Conference, and attended the dinner party by the Religious Affairs Bureau under the State

Council. Since then intercourse and exchange among Mainland Daoist bodies and those of Hong Kong and Macao have continued.

Intercourse between Daoist Mainland groups and those of Taiwan started in 1988. Soon after reassuming work in 1980, CTA published *A Letter to Daoist Friends in Taiwan*, expressing the Mainland Daoists' missing of Daoist friends across the straits and extended invitations to them, welcoming them to make pilgrimages to Mainland temples, exchange understanding of teaching, increase friendship and contribute to the re-union of the motherland.

◎ A religious delegation from Taiwan during its visit to White Cloud Temple in Beijing.

In April 1988, a delegation of six persons headed by Long Jinlian, the Vice President of Fuyou Palace in Southern Taiwan, visited Eight Immortals Palace in Xi°an, Shaanxi Province, and entreated the transfer of one duplicate of Lu Dongbin's statue to Taiwan, which was worshipped by 50,000 believers at the consecration celebration in Taiwan.

On August 2, 1988, a delegation of 26 pilgrims from Cisheng Palace in central Taiwan arrived at the Celestial Master's Mansion in Jiangxi Province to pay their homage to the ancient temple. The two daughters and one nephew (Zhang Jintao, who is now the president of the Mansion) of the 36th generation Celestial

◎ The Shanghai Daoist Association prays for world peace.

◎ A Japanese delegation from the World Religions and Peace Committee visits CTA in October 2002.

Master Zhang Enfu received them. This delegation also entreated the transfer of two duplicate statues of Zhang Daoling to Taiwan.

On August 8, 1989, a delegation of 15 persons from the China Daoist Association in Taiwan, headed by its Deputy Secretary-general, Zhangsheng, visited CTA, and expressed their good wishes to enhance mutual friendship. Zhangsheng said: "No matter what happens, the intercourse among Daoists of Taiwan and Mainland should not break off, because we have the same founder. Only by believing in Daoism and only by purity, calm and non-artificial striving, can Chinese people lead happy lives."

On the 19th of the same month, a delegation from Gaoxiong

Culture Institute and Taoyuan Mingsheng Daoist Monastery in Taiwan visited Master Lao's Cave in Chongqing, also expressing their wishes to enhance their relationship with Mainland Daoist bodies. They said that: "The roots of Daoism are in the Mainland. It is our long wish to return to the Mainland and search our roots. We will come back again for pilgrimages."

Since the 1990s, CTA also has sent delegations to Taiwan to visit, give lectures, attend celebrations, hold ceremonies and perform musical rituals.

CTA also has had friendly intercourse with foreign Daoist

◎ The former President of Austria during his visit to White Cloud Temple.

organizations and scholastic institutes. In the 1950s-60s, the famous Japanese Sinologist Fukunaga Mitsuji visited CTA several times. In 1959, the famous British

◎ The former Chancellor of Germany, Helmut Kohl, during his visit to White Cloud Temple.

Sinologist, Joseph Needham, visited White Cloud Temple in Beijing and discussed alchemy with the famous Daoist scholar and President of CTA, Chen Yingning.

In the 1980s, CTA established friendly relationships with more Daoist bodies in the world, among which the most important are the French Daoist Association, the Singapore Daoist Association, the Institute of Oriental Culture under the University of Tokyo, the Three Pure Ones Temple in Malaysia, Zhongfu Daoist Temple in Arizona, Zigeng Temple in San Francisco, Taixuan Temple in Hawaii. the Taoist Taiqi Society, and Fung Loy Kok Institute of Taoism in Toronto.

At the beginning of this century, CTA has established friendly relationships with Daoist bodies, disciples and scholars in about 30 countries, sent 27 delegations of 230 persons in total

◎ The President of CTA, Min Zhiting, during a Daoist Festival at Mount Mian, Shanxi Province.

to more than 10 countries, received 360 visiting groups of 35,000 persons, which include some large names, such as the German Chancellor, Kohl, and the American, Henry Kissinger.

In September, 1993, from the 17th to the 26th, the Daoist bodies of the Mainland, Taiwan and Hong Kong jointly held the Great Sacrificial Ceremony for Luotian (Luotian Dajiao) at White Cloud Temple in Beijing, themed as "Praying for Peace for World, Country and People". Luotian is the Daoist name for Empyrean or highest heaven, which surpass the Three Realms of Desire, Material and Spirit. Jiao was the archaic sacrificial ceremony for Heaven, adopted by Daoism; Zhai was the ceremony to appeal for Heaven's help. After the Sui Dynasty, Zhai and Jiao were used together to refer to all Daoist sacrificial ceremonies (sometimes abbreviated as Jiao). The Great Jiao is the long lasting ceremonies.

This Luotian Dajiao was chaired by the President of CTA, Fu Yuantian, and co-chaired by Hou Baoyuan, Abbot of Hong Kong Ching Chung Koon Temple, Gao Zhongxin, the Abbot of Taipei Zhinan Palace, and Huang Xinyang, the Deacon of White Cloud Temple in Beijing. There were installed 1200 statues of deities in 10 shrines. The participants were White Cloud Temple

ⓒ Great Purity Palace, Mount Lao, Shandong Province.

◎ The Vice President, Xie Zongxin, and Deputy Secretary-General, Zhang Jiyu, present during the World Summit of Religions and Conservation in London, 1994.

in Beijing, Hong Kong Qingsong Daoist Temple, Taipei Zhinan Palace, White Cloud Temple in Shanghai, Xuanmiao Temple in Suzhou, Baopu Daoist Temple in Hangzhou, Mount Wudang Daoist Association, Eight Immortals Palace in Xi'an, Mount Qingcheng Daoist Association, Sanyuan Palace in Guangzhou, Fung Ying Sin Koon in Hong Kong, Xingshan Daoist Temple in Hong Kong, and some Daoist temples in the United States, Canada and Australia. The participants included some foreign Daoists from Singapore, Malaysia, Japan, Korea and France.

This Luotian Dajiao received donations amounting to one

 Daoism in China

million RMB, all of which were subsequently donated to "Hope Project", which is the national education foundation for poor, general rural, populations in China.

From May 21st to 30th, 2001, CTA co-hosted the second Luotian Dajiao, in association with the Shanxi Daoist Association and Jiexiu City Daoist Association in Shanxi Province, the theme of which was "Praying for World Peace, State Prosperity, Motherland Reunion and Happiness". There were 15 shrines installed by the Daoist bodies from Beijing, Shanghai, Jiangxi, Jiangsu, Sichuan, Hubei, Shanxi, Shaanxi, Northeast China, Hong Kong, Macao, Taiwan, Singapore and Korea. More than 300 performers took part.

◎ The Daoist Orchestra of Suzhou during its performance tour (UK).

From August 28 to 31, 2000, the President of CTA, Min
Zhiting, and six other leaders of the five major Chinese religions
presented the Millennium World Peace Summit of Religious and
Spiritual Leaders, held in the headquarters of the UN. He made a
prayer speech at the opening celebration in the name of Daoism.
He prayed for world peace, harmonious co-existence and
intimacy like that of family members. He also expressed wishes
for China's reunion, peace, stability, and ethnic and religious
harmony. He said: "The ecological crisis today is closely related
to the egocentric values and the incessant exploitative thinking
patterns of human beings that have brought about great damages
to nature. The hi-tech wars that assume biochemical and nuclear
weapons are especially threatening to both human life and its
environment. Hence our Daoists advocate that: (1) only by
changing our attitudes to nature, recognizing the unity between
man and nature, and following the way of nature can we realize
sustainable development; (2) respect life, control desire, do not
kill animals and expand our benevolence to all creatures; (3)
stop any war and resolve disputes by negotiation, stop any damage
to the environment and live in natural ways." These views were
greatly appreciated and welcomed by people all over the world
who love peace and nature.

From March 17th to 20th, 2003, CTA launched and hosted the Grand Anniversary Celebration of Laozi's Birth, which comprised sacrificial ceremonies, memorial conferences, calligraphy and painting demonstrations as well as Daoist concerts. The representatives came from various local Daoist organizations in Mainland China, Hong Kong, Macao and Taiwan, as well as Singapore and Malaysia. Reverend Min Zhiting said that the purpose of the memorial celebration of Laozi was to spread and carry on his doctrines of "respecting Dao and its Virtue", "imitating nature", "being benevolent and tolerant", "doing good and summoning good", and "being thrifty, not excessive", and thereby promoting the development of Daoism. The art exhibition along with the concert enhanced the ceremony's cultural value. The concerts were performed by Daoist Orchestras of White Cloud Temple in Beijing, Mount Mao in Jiangsu, Xuanmiao Temple in Suzhou, Mount Mian in Shanxi, the Hong Kong Penglai Daoist Temple, Gaoxiong Culture Institute, the Wall and Moat God Temple in Singapore, and the Choir of the *Daode Jing* of Dashibo Palace in Singapore.

© Mount Mian, Shanxi.

CHAPTER 8
THE INFLUENCE OF DAOISM

Daoism has inherited much from early Chinese culture, and for centuries interacted and often merged with Confucianism and Buddhism, becoming one of the major pillars of traditional Chinese culture. Thus the influence of Daoism surpasses the circle of Daoist groups, and is an important factor in the molding of Chinese traits, methods of thought, and behavior.

1. The Influence of Daoism on Chinese Traditional Culture

We can find traces of Daoism in the cosmology, ethics, and aesthetics of traditional philosophy. Laozi's cosmology holding that one gave birth to two, two gave birth to three and three gave birth to the ten thousand things, has always been the dominating cosmology of Chinese people. The doctrines of correspondence between humans and the universe advocated by Daoism are still very much a part of the Chinese mentality. A lot of Chinese people believe that the changes of the celestial bodies influence social and personal trends, and reversibly social and personal behavior can cause fluctuation in the universe. Daoist moral norms of wuwei, purity, nature, the control of desire, thriftiness, yielding, benevolence and harmony are important components of traditional morality. Daoist pursuit of immortality on the basis of reality had great influence on Chinese aesthetics, for example "returning to the origin and embracing simplicity", and "wordless beauty". These ideas and feelings have been passed on for tens

◎ Statue Consecration at Five Dragon Palace (Mount Qian, Liaoning).

of centuries, and have become the spiritual characteristics and identity of China.

Daoism has also contributed greatly to Chinese medicine. Although the ultimate goal of Daoism is to identify with Dao and become immortal, the cultivation of the body and medical methods in pursuit of longevity are necessary as preconditions. Hence Daoism has made use of medicine and often led the way in Chinese medicine. Daoist ideas of "treating before illness"and "consolidating life foundation" made Chinese medicine put prevention at the forefront. The "vital energy theory" of Daoist cosmology is the basic principle of both Daoist cultivation and

Chinese medicine. Some Daoist classics are also very important medical treatises, such as *The Internal Classic of the Yellow Emperor*, *Synopsis Of Prescriptions Of The Golden Chamber* and *Collection of Commentaries on the Divine Farmer's Classic of Medicinal Herbs*. Many Daoist masters of history were also great doctors, such as Gehong, Tao Hongjin and Sun Simiao.

Daoism has also been closely related to Chinese arts. First of all, the aesthetic values of Daoism, as referred to above, are an intrinsic part of Chinese arts. The celestial world and transcendent images are key components of Chinese arts. The images of running or flying divine birds and animals fill the decorations on excavated bronze ware from the fifth to third century BCE. The work of Wang Yanshou, an artist of

◎ Daoist disciples offering joss sticks.

the Western Han Dynasty, depicted immortals, fairy maidens, red phoenixes, as well as Fuxi, the hero-ancestor who took the body of Kylin, and Nuwa, who is the heroine-ancestor with the body of snake. After religious Daoism came into being in the second century AD, paintings of immortal stories and Daoist teachings played a greater part in Chinese art. Some of these works are of great artistic value, such as those of Gu Kaizhi (345-406

◎ The Gods of the Big Dipper.

AD) of the Wei and Jin Dynasty, Wu Daozi of the Tang Dynasty, and Emperor Huizong (1082-1135) of the Southern Song Dynasty.

Sculptures of deities and the frescoes of Daoist temples hold a high status in Chinese art history. The extant Daoist statues from the seventh to ninth century include the statue of the

Heavenly Sage of Changyang preserved in the Shanxi Provincial Museum, the statue of Laozi from the Tang Dynasty, preserved in the Shaanxi Provincial Museum, and the statues of Jade Maiden Spring Grotto, Mianyang City, Sichuan Province. Those from the 11th to 14th century are the Giant Statue of Laozi at Qingliang Mountain, Chuanzhou, Fujian, the Grotto of Mount Shiquan in Sichuan, the Southern Mountain Grotto in Dazu, Sichuan, the Handmaiden's Statue of the Holy Mother's Hall in Taiyuan, Shanxi, the statues in Two Immortals' Temple and Jade Emperor's Temple in Jincheng, Shanxi, and the Statues of the Three Pure Ones in Xuanmiao Temple in Suzhou, Jiangsu. Those after the 14th century are the Dragon Mountain's Grottoes in Taiyuan, Shanxi, the statue of the Water God Temple in Hongdong,

◎ A picuture of Laozi on a black ox by Zhanglu, a Ming dynasty artist.

Shanxi, the statues of the Twenty Eight Constellations in Jincheng, Shanxi, the statues of Sacred Aunt's Temple in Gaoping, Shanxi, and the statues of Guandi's Temple in Jiezhou, Shanxi.

The most important Daoist temple frescos are those of the Eastern Sacred Mountain's Temple in Tai'an,

◎ Embroidered Flags from the Qing Dynasty, (White Cloud Temple, Beijing).

Shandong, the Northern Sacred Mountain's Temple in Quyang, Hebei, Eternal Happiness Temple in Ruicheng, Shanxi, and Water God's Temple in Hongdong, Shanxi. These are art treasures of both China and the world. From November 2000 to January 2001, the Art Institute of Chicago hosted a show on "Taoism and the Arts of China" in Chicago and San Francisco. At that time more than 150 articles concerning Daoist sculptures and paintings were presented, and more than 100,000 people attended. A symposium on the same topic was held in the early days of the exhibition.

Daoist music has greatly influenced Chinese classical music. Daoism has inherited early beliefs, along with liturgical songs, spells, charms, dances, bells, drums and other music elements. The standard Daoist musical system started around 415 AD, when Kou Qianzhi declared that he had been instructed by Master Lao to institute Daoist liturgies and published *New Musical Liturgy of Commandments from the Clouds*. The rhythms he adopted such as Huaxia Anthems and Buxu Chants were recomposed from the court music of the Qin and Han

© Daoist Martial Art, Bagua Quan (Eight-Trigrams Boxing).

Dynasties. In later dynasties, Daoism has continued to draw from court music, some of which were the works of famous Daoist emperors such as Tang Emperor Xuanzong and Song Emperor Huizong, while another important influence was folk music of various regions in different periods. Thus there are some

第 三 届 道 教 音 乐 汇 演

◎ Daoist Liturgical Music Performance, March 18, 2003.

common rhythms such as Shifang Rhythms followed by all temples, and some are local rhythms, which are used only in temples in a given region, for example, Shaanxi Rhythms, Beijing Rhythms, and Wenzhou Rhythms.

Daoist music is played in religious liturgies, and has specific uses as well as profound philosophical meaning. It is closely related to folk custom, popular with people, and a treasure house for the study of ancient Chinese folk music. There have been three large scale activities of collecting, editing and studying Daoist music in the PRC: in the 1950s these activities were mostly carried out in Southeast China, from which emerged some important works such as *The Moon Reflected on the Second Springs* which is the well known erhu solo by the blind Daoist musician, Abing, as well as some books, such as *A Report on Religious Music Survey in Hunan, An Introduction to Daoist Music in Yangzhou* and *Collection of Daoist Art in Suzhou*. During the 1970s and 1980s the second research project worked with sound, score, chart, text and visual images, and studied historical changes, forms and characteristics of Daoist music. In the 1980s a third research project was conducted independently in Beijing, Shanghai, Suzhou, Wuhan, Mount Wudang, Mount Qianshan in Liaoning,,and Mount Lao in Shandong, which produced many papers and records. In June 1990, TCI and the Music Institute of the Chinese Art Academy co-hosted the Symposium on Chinese Daoist Music. After that, the Daoist Orchestra organized by Daoist bodies, visited and performed in Venice, Florence, Rome, Toronto, Kuala Lumpur, Mali, Singapore, Hong Kong and Taiwan, and held open concerts at the Beijing Odeum, all of which received praise from musical circles home and abroad.

2. The Influence of Daoism on Folk Customs and Minorities

Daoism has great influence on the daily life of Chinese people. Some of the prevailing holidays came from Daoism, but their meanings have changed over the course of history.

The current annual Festival of Lanterns on the fifteenth day of the first moon, during which every family hangs lanterns, eats dumplings and participates in lantern festivals, was the Daoist holiday of Superior Principles Day, originally on the fifth day of the first moon prescribed by the Daoist founder Zhang Daoling, dedicated to the god of the Celestial Element. However the custom of hanging lanterns and going to the lantern fairs, as Song Dynasty scholars have proved, was initiated by Han Emperor Wu, whose purpose was to offer sacrifice to the North Pole God (Taiyi) all through the night on the fifteenth day of the same moon. To do so lanterns were used in the festival. The present custom is the synthesis of these two customs.

Tomb-Sweeping Day (Qingming Jie literally means the

◎ Temple Fair during Spring Festival at White Cloud Temple. People were touching the monkey sculptures to pray for good fortune for the coming year. There are three monkey sculptures in different places in the temple, which are believed to be capable of granting good fortune only to those who touched them all.

"Pure and Shining Day") on the fourth day of the third moon was transformed from the Cold Food Day and the Non-Smoke Day, which came from the story of Jie Zitui, according to scholars of the Song Dynasty. Jie Zitui was a hermit of the Jin State during the Spring-Autumn period. He had performed great deeds for the state, but refused to become an official, instead remaining on a mountain. In order to force him to come out, the Duke of Jin ordered to set fire to the forest of the mountain where he lived. But Jie Zitui would rather be burnt to death than obey the Duke's request. After he heard of this news, the Duke of Jin fell into deep sorrow and ordered all fires extinguished and that people eat only cold food in honor of this sage. Jie Zitui was subsequently deified by Daoism because of his transcendent deeds. There were annual memorial ceremonies on the 105th day after the Winter Solstice by stopping all fire, and hanging strings of date cakes on door lintel, which were threaded with wickers. In recent times, however, it has become the day for families to sweep tombs of their late relatives.

Dragon Boat Festival (Duanwu Jie or Duanyang Jie, literally means the first five days of the middle summer) is on the fifth day of the fifth moon, and was originally a Daoist holiday of

© Temple fair during Spring Festival (White Cloud Temple, Beijing).

exorcism. According to ancient books, whenever the day came, every family pasted a piece of paper on its door with the Celestial Master's image or talisman charmed with a red stamp in order to guard against any vagabond ghosts or deities. In later history people connected this festival with the story of Quyuan the patriotic and loyal minister of the state of Chu during the Spring-Autumn period who drowned himself to demonstrate his own will and disapproval of his duke. People now put rice dumplings into water to memorialize him. So it also a day of making glutinous rice dumplings wrapped in bamboo or reed leaves.

The Mid-Autumn Festival that is on the 15th day of the 8th moon was originally a Daoist holiday offering sacrifice to the Moon God, something inherited from early imperial sacrifice and celebration of an abundant harvest. Inspired by the poetic impression of the idea that "moon is round like cake", later generations have adopted the custom of making and eating moon cakes on the day.

The Double Ninth Festival is also called the Double Yang Festival because in Chinese odd numbers correspond to yang and the number nine is the largest single digit yang number. The festival comes from the story of the Daoist Priest, Fei Changfang, who saved the family of Huanjing. Huan followed Fei to cultivate Dao.

One day, Fei suddenly told Huan his family would suffer from a great disaster, and instructed him to hurry home, bind cornus officinalis ("Zhuyu" in Chinese, a kind of herb) wickers around the arm of his family members and take them to the mount of a hill and drink chrysanthemum wine.

◎　A Western Daoist disciple in meditation (Mount Lu, Jiangxi Province).

Huan did as Fei instructed. When the family returned home from the hill in the evening, they found all their domestic animals had died. Ever since then, it has become a day of climbing mountains and drinking; females of old also wore a bag of cornus officinalis to guard against devils. Today it has transformed into the Day of Climbing Mountains, and because many elderly peoople climb and drink on that day, which is regarded to be beneficial to their health and longevity, it is also called Elders' Day.

Moreover, the custom of pasting pictures of gods on

household doors, lighting firecrackers and so on, originated from stories or beliefs related to Daoism.

Religious Daoism adopted many religious elements of minorities in Southwest China, such as Di, Qiang, Yu, Pu, Qiongmian, Mosha and Kunming. For example, the central practice of "charmed water" probably came from witchcraft of these tribes. Conversely, after its foundation, the Daoist religion became the beliefs of many minorities. According to estimations, at least 10 of the 60 million people belonging to the 55 minorities of China maintain Daoist beliefs.

◎ The Performers of Rites of Zhinan Palace in Taipei parade for the Heavenly Sages.

The Kitchen God is commonly worshipped in the families of the Achang nationality, living in Yunnan; temples dedicated to the Jade Emperor, the Wall and Moat God, as well as Guandi can be found in their towns.

The Jing nationality, living in Guangxi, mostly worship the Daoist constellation gods, such as the Gods of the Sexagenary Cycle, the Thirty-Six Celestial Gods of the Big Dipper, and the Seventy-Two Earthly Gods of the Big Dipper. The Daoist priests there belong to the Zhengyi Denomination, who assume the father-son succession and do not need to inhabit monasteries.

The Maonan nationality, living in Guangxi, believe in an eclectic religion that merges Daoist beliefs and customs with their tribal religion, called the Meishan Sect.

The Tu nationality, living mainly in Qinghai, takes Zhenwu (the God of War or Northern God) and the Empyrean Lady (or the Mystic Lady of the Highest Heaven) as their central objects of worship. They hold grand temple fairs on the Double Ninth Day every year for exorcisms and sacrificial ceremonies.

The Zhuang nationality, mostly living in Guangxi, also maintain many Daoist ideas along with their own ancient practice, and they take Supreme Master Lao as the highest god, along with the Jade Emperor, the Three Pure Ones, Zhenwu and the

Empyrean Lady.

The Uyghur people, mostly living in Xinjiang, had originally practiced Daoism as their religion before adopting Islam.

3. The Influence of Daoism on Chinese People Outside of China

In the past 100 years, Daoism has spread to five continents along with Chinese diasporas, mostly happening in the decades after 1940. Many Non-Chinese have also begun to convert to Daoism in the late 20th century. According to an incomplete 1989 estimation by an international religious organization, there were

◎　Western Daoist Monks parade for the Heavenly Sages.

◎ Daoist Monks from Sichuan Province in the consecration of a statue in Malaysia. Only after having been consecrated by monks can a statue have divinity. The consecration includes chanting and stroking the deity's eyes with cinnabar, amongst other rites.

Daoist believers or Daoist bodies in about 65 countries. According to Chinese scholar Zheng Tianxing's paper *Occidental Daoist Studies and the Spread of Daoism in Foreign Countries*, in countries outside of China, there were 31.28 million Daoist believers, and more than 600 Daoist temples.   Most of the activity was in Asia, though there were estimated to be 25,000 believers and 54 temples in North America, 27,000 believers and 85 temples in South America, 29,000 believers and 98 temples in Europe, 3,400 believers and 54 temples in Africa, 9,500 believers and 130 temples in Oceania, 3,400 believers and 12 temples in

Japan, 5,200 believers and 9 temples in Thailand, 2,700 believers and 7 temples in Burma, 820 believers and 4 temples in Indonesia, 120 believers and 2 temples in India, and 38,000 believers and 198 temples in Singapore.

图书在版编目（CIP）数据

中国道教／王宜峨著；曾传辉译．—北京：五洲传播出版社，2004.10
（中国宗教基本情况丛书）

ISBN 7-5085-0598-0

Ⅰ.中... Ⅱ.①王... ②曾... Ⅲ.道教史－中国－英文 Ⅳ.B959.2

中国版本图书馆 CIP 数据核字（2004）第 101766 号

《中国道教》

责任编辑：荆孝敏

编辑助理：蔡　程

图片提供：王宜峨　谢　军　汪传树等

设计承制：北京紫航文化艺术有限公司

翻　　译：曾传辉

审　　校：〔美〕程子文

《中国道教》

五洲传播出版社

地址：中国北京北三环中路 31 号　邮编：100088

电话：82008174　网址：www.cicc.org.cn

开本：140 × 210 1/32　印张：7.1

2004 年 10 月第一版　印数 1-7000

ISBN 7-5085-0598-0/B·44

定价：48.00元